NO EXCUSES

Aimee Walker Rondo ♡

No Excuses

THE STORY OF ELITE GYMNAST AIMEE WALKER-POND

Adam U. Kempler

Impact Publishing, LLC
Santa Clarita, California

For information, contact Impact Publishing, LLC:
Email: Info@Impact-Publishing.com
Website: www.impact-publishing.com.

Library of Congress Control Number: 2015911285
Kempler, Adam U.
No Excuses: The Story of Elite Gymnast Aimee Walker-Pond

ISBN 978-0-9817794-6-1

Cover photograph courtesy of UCLA Athletics
Cover design by Rachel Robinson

We express appreciation for permission to print photographs from several sources: Lorin Hadlock,
GK Elite Sportswear, Rafael Beer, University of California, Los Angeles, and Brigham Young
University.

Printed in the United States of America

10 9 8 7 6 5 4 3 2

Contents

This book is dedicated to all people who are facing physical and mental challenges and to the community that supports them.

Preface

"The best time to plant a tree is twenty years ago. The second best time is now," says one Chinese proverb. When I started this project, I had no idea that it would take thirteen years to complete and involve about eighty interviews with Aimee's family, friends, mentors, and coaches. Why did it take so long? When I first met Aimee, I was an English professor, and she was in the middle of her career. No one knew how long her career would take or where it would take her; however, I could see that her story was significant and had to be told, so I approached Aimee about writing her story. We then agreed to work together on this project—although at the time we didn't fully understand the place her story would take in the gymnastics world and in disability literature.

Helen Keller said, "Blindness cuts us off from things, but deafness cuts us off from people." Most of us don't have much experience with blindness, deafness, or other disabilities. When I was working my way through college, the only job I could get was working with severely handicapped students as an instructional aide at a high school, which I reluctantly accepted out of financial desperation. I worked with a young man who had been a popular running back on the school's football team but had been hit head-on by a drunk driver, placing him in the severely handicapped program. When I first saw him, he was drooling in a wheelchair, and I felt sick to my stomach. After four years of working together, he became one of my best friends. Through that experience and many others like it, I gained a better understanding of some of the struggles that others face, and it prepared me to see the significance of Aimee's story when I first heard about it.

After twenty-seven years in prison, Nelson Mandela said, "As I walked out the door toward the gate that would lead to my freedom, I knew if I didn't leave my bitterness and hatred behind, I'd still be in prison." People with disabilities are imprisoned by their bodies, and most of them are never set free in this life. I taught a class in a juvenile detention facility for five years, and I had a student who stopped me outside of class one day. She looked across the grass at the tall fence at the end of the field. It was wrapped with razor wire at the top. She said, "I can't take it in here. I've got nine months left, and I can't handle being away from my family." Being incarcerated can change us, and by teaching in detention camps, I gained a better understanding of the need that we all have for hope, especially the disenfranchised. I hope that readers of Aimee's biography will gain a better understanding of the world of people with disabilities and encourage others to feel hopeful.

1 Not a Ballerina

Aimee flawlessly executed the round-off whip-back handspring into a two and a half twist. At the exact moment that she took her final pose—on her knees with her body arched back and hands in the air—the music from *Carmen* ended.

She hopped up and turned to salute the Russian judges, both arms raised, with mannequin hands. Her blond ponytail hung still, but the diamonds on her power-red leotard sparkled.

Is it enough? she thought, holding her breath.

The audience then exploded, jumping to its feet, clapping and cheering; not one person remained seated.

Aimee jumped up and down—making little claps at her chest—unable to conceal her delight, and she blew kisses to the crowd.

Reporters had spread the word through papers and television that an American had overcome all odds to compete at the international elite meet, and people from all over had come to Kazakhstan to the Nellie Kim International Invitational to see if the stories were true.

Aimee marched back to her coach, Hal, with a prayer of

gratitude in her heart. The cheering continued, so Hal gently pushed her back onto the floor to acknowledge the applause.

Then, Nellie Kim, five-time Olympic gold medalist, emerged from the crowd, walked out to Aimee, drew a big heart on her chest and pointed to Aimee to communicate, "I love you." She hugged Aimee and gave her a bouquet of flowers.

With goosebumps and tearful eyes, Aimee smiled, feeling the love and joy that comes from being honored for doing your best.

Despite challenge after challenge and setback after setback, Aimee had achieved international success. This is her story.

At dusk, one week before Patsy Walker's third child was due, the Walker family gathered into the 1981 blue Honda Civic, the only new car the Walkers had ever purchased. They headed to Sav-On to purchase a few items, including a special treat: toy rewards for good behavior that Danny and Jamie had earned for helping to clean the house and for getting along. Patsy and the kids clicked their seatbelts, but Patsy felt divided about wearing one: it would provide protection for her, but in the event of an accident, it could also harm her unborn child.

Driving down Moorpark Street in Studio City, California, Cam, Patsy's husband, pulled into the left turn lane. A sedan stopped abruptly in front of him. Cam stomped on the brake, locking the wheels and jolting the car to a stop, just avoiding a crash. "What are you doing?" Cam yelled at the other driver. Danny and Jamie, 7 and 2, shrieked. Cam turned to Patsy. "Are you okay?" he asked.

"I think so," Patsy responded. She immediately feared her water would break and she would go into labor. "You need to be more careful," she said. Realizing it was not his fault, she turned to Danny and Jamie and said, "Are you boys okay? Don't be afraid. We're all fine."

"Bubby's okay," Danny said, referring to his little brother.

Patsy's main concern was her high-risk pregnancy and

scheduled VBAC—vaginal birth after Cesarean.

Being a doctor's son, Cam played down the event, but Patsy's fear had substance. Though her due date was still a week away, a sharp labor pain lasting thirty to forty seconds shot through her stomach and back. At Sav-On, she stayed in the car while Cam and the boys picked up what was needed. A second contraction rocked her body.

Her first labor, with Danny, had lasted thirty-seven hours. Dr. Smith had had time to complete a golf game before he finally became available to order a C-section.

Patsy's right shin began to throb. She reached for her leg and felt a little indentation where the underside of the dashboard had barely split her skin. Within a few minutes the bump had swelled half an inch, and she remembered that her own mother had gone into labor after suffering a leg wound in a car accident.

After Cam and the boys returned, the Walkers drove home slowly. Cam helped Patsy out of the car, past the cedar tree that dwarfed their 1,000 square foot home, through the door, and into an overstuffed armchair decorated in Renaissance tapestry. Cam pulled over a wooden stool, and Patsy propped her feet up and began to think.

Patsy had first realized just how small her house was when she discovered she could vacuum the entire two-bedroom house from one electrical outlet. From the street, any passerby could see a red brick house and two sets of white French doors, one on either side of the front door, which opened onto the front porch. Despite the size and simplicity of the house, the Walkers felt they had a special home. Years later, after Jamie had visited a friend's mansion, he would tell Patsy, "Mom, I love our home. It's sacred." All the Walkers felt that way.

Patsy's father, Skee, came to their home to help Cam give a priesthood blessing to support her in the delivery of her child. As Patsy sat in a chair, Skee stood behind her and anointed her head with holy oil. Then Cam and Skee placed their hands on Patsy's head, and Cam offered a prayer.

Patsy's worries stemmed from her prior pregnancies, two of

which concluded in C-sections. With both Danny and Jamie, Patsy felt nauseous for about half of each pregnancy. Between Danny and Jamie, Patsy had two miscarriages, one when she was five months along and had to deliver in the hospital, where she passed out, and required both a D & C (removal of tissue) and a blood transfusion. After Jamie's birth, Patsy needed another blood transfusion because she was anemic and lost a lot of blood.

But Patsy's main concern sprang from her current pregnancy, which included a kidney infection during the second trimester, requiring several antibiotics. And unlike Patsy's pregnancy with her two boys, this nausea had lasted throughout the entire pregnancy. Every week for thirty-seven weeks, Patsy would get sick from the smell of food and spices like garlic, onion, veggie salt, brownies, meat, and eggs. All she could eat was unbuttered popcorn, diluted chicken noodle soup (only the Lipton brand), watered-down Postum, and dry toast without butter.

Ironically, during this pregnancy, the smell of gasoline and tires appealed to her, and she craved to inhale these fragrances. She also craved the earthy smell of rocks and dirt—to the point where she asked Danny to find marble-sized rocks from the garden, which she sucked on—without cleaning first. Before her pregnancy, Patsy, 5'2", weighed 106 pounds. By the third month, due to nausea, she had dropped to 98 pounds, and by the end of the pregnancy, she weighed a mere 117 pounds.

The smell of food made her so sick that she would roll up toilet paper into little tubes and insert them into her nose to block the odors that induced vomiting. She had to do this even when she went to eat dinner at her parents' home.

At that time, Cam loved brownies, and he could eat an entire pan full. He would stay up late and do the laundry and watch TV. He would wait until 1:00 a.m. when he was sure that Patsy slept soundly, and then he would make brownies, sometimes a hamburger and brownies. He would open the door that led from their bedroom to the fresh air outdoors and close the bedroom door to prevent the smell of food from wafting in from the kitchen. The aroma, however, would always drift under the door and wake Patsy up. Patsy had heard on the news about a woman who threatened her husband if he didn't stop drinking, and Patsy used the same line on Cam: "When you're asleep, I'm going to sew you up in the sheets and whack you with a bat if you don't stop it." Then, Patsy would rush to the bathroom to throw up. After Cam would apologize, they would open all the doors and windows in the house, trying to rid their home of the savory odors so Patsy could fall back asleep.

Also, during Patsy's second trimester and much of the third, the baby lay transverse and moved much less than the boys had. Because the baby lay transverse, the sonogram results were inconclusive about the child's gender, but Patsy expected a boy because she had two boys already. Although the Walkers had considered girl names, they had settled on Cody Glen for their third boy.

In Cam's priesthood blessing, he did not promise an end to her problems but said that everything would work out for their good. He said the doctors would know how to address the situation, that everything would be fine, including the boys, and that they all would be in good hands—that their Father in Heaven was going to take care of everything.

Cam called his father, Dr. Walker, who listened to Cam's description of Patsy's condition.

"Just keep us apprised," he said.

Cam also called Dr. Judd Goodman, Patsy's obstetrician, who claimed that Patsy was his favorite patient. "No problem," said Dr. Goodman. "This is very important to me. Remind Patsy to relax. Just go to the hospital, and when everything is ready, I'll be right over."

The Walkers joined in a family prayer, and their excitement for a new family member grew as Patsy's contractions became stronger, although the timing remained inconsistent.

She slept little while her contractions gained momentum. By 4:30 a.m., Patsy knew they should go to the hospital, and she started checking everything. Patsy had arranged for her mother, Lyle, to come over to watch the boys while she and Cam went to the hospital. She called her mom at about 5:45 a.m.

Patsy felt comforted that her mother was there to watch her boys. Lyle said, "I love you, little Patsy. The boys will be fine. You don't have to worry about a thing. I'm so sorry you have to go through this, but what an unbelievable result. Nothing is more precious than those babies, and we're so excited. We just can't wait." Lyle lifted her shoulders and clenched her fists and smiled, making Patsy feel like her delivery was the most important thing in the world.

As the Walkers were leaving, Lyle said to Cam, "Don't you leave us out. We want to know every single thing that's happening." Out of Lyle's nine children, seven were girls, and Patsy was the only one who had had a C-section—and two at that—but Lyle masked her concern.

Both Patsy and Lyle cried and hugged each other.

The Walkers drove to the hospital without incident.

After checking in, a hospital worker took Patsy by wheelchair to a labor room for high-risk pregnancies. One bed rested against the wall, and Patsy saw much more equipment than she could recall from her prior labor rooms. She dreaded the Pitocin drip from memories of the drug accelerating Danny's delivery. The nurse set up the fetal heart monitor, connecting it directly to the baby's head in utero.

Half an hour after arriving at the hospital, Dr. Goodman's nurse said, "He is on his way to the hospital and has canceled his appointments for the day."

At one of Patsy's recent appointments, Dr. Goodman had explained, "The baby appears to be small enough to deliver vaginally, but don't worry. I won't let you go more than one hour at any one centimeter, and if there is any sign of stress or struggle, we are all set up to take the baby Cesarean if necessary." Dr. Goodman continued, "I don't want you to worry. We are looking out for both of you, but I want you to have the opportunity to deliver the baby vaginally if at all possible." Dr. Goodman and his partner were publishing a work on VBACs, and their ideas were influencing delivery practices.

In fact, Dr. Goodman had just delivered two VBACs successfully the week before, and his enthusiasm for VBAC deliveries showed. He said that he would delegate his other responsibilities and would be there all day for Patsy.

Cam stayed in the room. Since they had attended classes for the Bradley method of delivery, a natural childbirth process, prior to the birth of their first child, Cam felt prepared to support Patsy in the birth of their children.

When Dr. Goodman arrived about forty-five minutes later, he greeted them and assured them that all would be okay. He brought in the nurses and explained to everyone that the baby's heart monitor had to stay between 110 and 150. The head nurse of the obstetrics floor looked nervous and said to the doctor, "We shouldn't take any chances here."

The doctor assured her that everything would be just fine and not to worry because he would be there until the baby was born, regardless of how long it took. It was that important to him. Dr. Goodman explained that if the heart rate fell below 110, he was to be notified immediately. "As long as the heart rate stays at this level and Patsy is comfortable," he said, "we are going to be fine."

Cam fixated on the printout of the fetal heart monitor, and he and Patsy both felt concerned about trying a VBAC. The doctor came in every twenty minutes or so, checked on Patsy, and left. About an hour and a half after Dr. Goodman's initial instructions, the baby's heart rate suddenly plummeted below 110 and stayed low for a couple of minutes.

Cam paced the floor, brushing back his hair with his hands. "The heart rate is too low," he said. "Where is the doctor?" Realizing he was alarming Patsy, he tried to appear calm.

He went to the door to try to catch a nurse's attention, but he saw no one. Then he said a little prayer, asking Heavenly Father to let him know if he needed to do something. Cam felt like he did need to tell people what was happening. Not wanting to worry Patsy, he said, "I'm just going to go down and ask Dr. Goodman a quick question. I'll be right back." Then he hustled to find Dr. Goodman: "The baby's heart rate has gone down, and I tried to get someone's attention." Dr. Goodman jumped up and ran down the hall to Patsy; Cam and the head nurse followed. In the labor room, he calmly asked Patsy to shift a little. Then the heart rate rose. Cam took a breath of relief.

"Do you think that it will be a problem that the heart rate dropped?" Cam asked.

"I think she is going to be fine," Dr. Goodman replied. "I don't think there was any significant damage."

The nurse said, "I don't feel real comfortable with this now. I think that we should consider a C-section at this time."

"I appreciate what you are saying," Dr. Goodman responded, "but I assure you that right now everything is stable. If the heart rate drops down again, we will certainly do a C-section." From that point on, Dr. Goodman stayed very close.

The Pitocin advanced the labor. At around six centimeters, Patsy received an epidural, eliminating sensation from the waist down.

After about ten hours, the nurses rolled Patsy from the labor room to the delivery room, during which time the baby's heart rate temporarily dropped below 110 for a second time.

Unusually bright lights lit up the clean delivery room, and a delivery table rested in the middle of the room. Cam tried to be calm. The doctor stayed there the entire time; the nurse stood nearby. The doctor spoke slowly and deliberately to everyone, but the nurses around him still looked nervous. Tension filled the room. Patsy never progressed beyond 9 centimeters, but the delivery continued.

During her contractions, Patsy clenched Cam's fingers and screamed.

As the baby was delivered, it came sunny-side up. The doctor said, "Get me the forceps." When the forceps came out, an unasked question hung in the air: "Why risk a VBAC?" Cam instinctively backed up, despite the custom of encouraging fathers to participate.

At 3:34 p.m. on March 10, 1983, Patsy delivered her third

baby, just 6 pounds, 1.5 ounces. When Cam and Patsy first saw their baby, they noticed a little, limp, blue form. The baby wasn't moving much, and Cam could see it was a girl.

The umbilical cord was wrapped around the baby's neck three times, and the forceps had left scratches on the baby's forehead and near the eyes.

The baby looked dark from anoxia. Cam thought, That was a close one. Then he thought, Good. We have a girl.

When Patsy noticed that her third child was a girl, she cried and cried because she felt so thrilled. She thought, She is the most beautiful little thing I have ever seen in my life.

Cam and Patsy also saw that their baby didn't cry; she didn't make any sounds. This was odd because her boys were so much bigger and louder. Patsy thought, Well, that's the difference between boys and girls.

The nurses whisked the baby away.

Cam saw that something was not right because the nurses were caring for the baby much more attentively than nurses had cared for their newborn sons. Cam said, "Is everything going to be okay?"

"Everything is going to be fine," the doctor responded. With time, the baby turned pink, and the Walkers breathed a sigh of relief.

Both the baby and Patsy were running a fever and had to stay in the hospital for a week. The forceps had jabbed Patsy's bladder, requiring a catheter.

During their stay in the hospital, Cam and Patsy discussed names for their baby. Cam had served a mission in France and recalled how his scriptures referred to the Savior as "bien-aimé": well beloved. The term fit their feelings for their daughter, so they agreed on Aimee.

When Patsy's pediatrician, Dr. Barlow, a friend of the family, came in, Cam asked again if their baby was going to be okay. "She has ten toes and ten fingers, but she has a low APGAR score," Dr. Barlow replied.

"What's that?" Patsy said.

He explained it as an assessment of the baby's overall health and said, "She should be okay, but I'm concerned that she may have difficulty sucking, and she has low muscle tone."

"What does that mean?" Patsy said.

"It means that she's floppy," said Dr. Barlow.

"And what does *that* mean?" Patsy replied.

"Well, it means that she probably won't be a ballerina." On the same note, he added, "She probably won't be a rocket scientist either." He continued, "You can live with that, can't you?"

"Oh, are you kidding? Of course. Is my baby okay?" Patsy persisted.

"She's just fine," he said. "Just watch her. We'll be watching her."

2 A Name and a Blessing

When Patsy lifted Aimee into her car seat to go home from the hospital, Aimee cried for the first time.

At home, Patsy would lift Aimee up to hold her upright against her chest, but Aimee would just cry and cry, arching her back as though she was in terrible pain. Then Patsy would lay her down on a pillow like she was a little princess, and she would be fine.

For the first three or four days, Aimee had to drink from a bottle because breastfeeding was too difficult. Then she progressed slowly and began nursing well.

That's all that the Walkers knew about Aimee's health on the first Sunday in May 1983, when Cam gave their daughter a name and a blessing at their church, The Church of Jesus Christ of Latter-day Saints. He blessed Aimee that she would be a light to the world and that others would learn through her because of her example and her spirit. He blessed her to grow up and increase in wisdom and be strong in mind, body, and spirit and to stay close to family and teachers. He blessed her to be a leader to those around her, an example, kind and loving. He blessed her to be righteous and find a worthy mate to marry in the temple. Cam blessed her with a special compassion that would draw others to her and allow her to touch others.

When Aimee was three-and-a-half months old, Patsy took her in for a check-up and immunization shots and to explain some of her concerns to the doctor, who checked Aimee and said, "She has congenital hip dysplasia, no hip sockets; they haven't formed yet."

"Are you sure?" Patsy asked in disbelief.

Even though the Walkers were on their way that day to a family reunion in Waterton, Canada, the doctor sent Patsy immediately to an orthopedic surgeon, Saul Bernstein, an expert in the field. He took x-rays that confirmed that neither hip sheath had formed.

At first, Dr. Bernstein thought that Aimee would need surgery because there was no sheath whatsoever. However, he wanted to try something else first, a hip brace, which Aimee had to wear twenty-four hours a day for six months and then only at night for a year. Aimee started to wear the brace the day they left for Waterton. It forced her legs into the splits position, with a bar separating her legs so the sockets around the balls could form. The brace consisted of buckles, joints, screws, and white nylon straps with cotton padding, making changing diapers very difficult, and baths almost impossible.

On the first of July, snow fell in Waterton. The weather aggravated Aimee's respiratory problems, which had started when she was six weeks old. Aimee coughed the entire time.

When the Walkers returned from Canada, the doctor x-rayed Aimee's hips once a week to see if the cartilage or sheath was beginning to form. If the sheath did not form, surgery would be required.

Between six weeks and six months, Aimee's respiratory problems continued. Patsy would take Aimee into the bathroom and turn the hot water on to create steam—until they later purchased a vaporizer. At six months, Aimee still couldn't sit up, so clearing her lungs and healing proved almost impossible.

Patsy didn't know what to do.

Late one morning in early November, Patsy left Cam with the kids so she could run some errands alone. Danny and Jamie were running back and forth through the kitchen and in and out of other rooms, yelping and screaming, and slamming doors along the way. Cam had gotten after them a couple of times about making so much noise and disturbing Aimee. She was nine months old, and Cam had set her in her seat on the floor in the kitchen, reclining a little on her back, playing with toys in her lap. Cam started to wash the dishes. As he was washing a pot's silver lid, it started to slip out of his hands, and he bobbled for it a couple of times, trying to ensure that it wouldn't fall on or startle Aimee. The lid sailed through the air, crashing on the floor a few inches behind Aimee, making a huge reverberating clank.

He braced himself for Aimee's startled reaction and yelled, "Oh, Aimee," but he noticed that Aimee didn't miss a beat; she had no reaction at all. She didn't move her head or her hands; she didn't flinch. She kept playing. When she didn't look at Cam, Cam realized something at once—as if someone had thrown a hot bucket of water over him—Aimee made no connection with what had happened. Cam yelled out a couple more times, "Aimee! Aimee!" She kept playing.

He picked the soapy lid off the floor, grabbed a second lid, stood behind Aimee, and banged them together like symbols: no response. He repeated the test, making even more noise: no reaction. He said, "That's not possible." He tried it again: nothing. Cam thought, She's deaf. Oh, my gosh. She's deaf. Where is Patsy?

Cam had no way to contact Patsy by phone, and each minute seemed like an hour.

He picked Aimee up and held her close to his chest and started pacing. His mind raced. She's deaf. This can't be happening to us. How can we deal with this? How am I going to break this to Patsy? Please, no, God, this can't be true. What are we going to do? Why would this happen to her?

Cam tried to picture Aimee's future life without sound, in addition to all of her other health problems. How will she understand music? How will she learn? How will she communicate with us? How will she date and marry? How will Danny and Jamie react?

Cam paced through every room in the house, running his hands through his hair, talking out loud to God, as the sun's rays fell through the windows and French doors on that particularly bright day. The boys ran through the living room.

"Knock it off!" shouted Cam, but then he stopped himself.

As he paced and consoled Aimee, he realized that she couldn't hear his words, which pained him and made him hug her more closely so she could feel his love through his embrace. He felt anxious and numb. Every thirty seconds or so, he looked out the front door.

After what seemed like hours—but which was only about twenty-five minutes—Patsy returned home with a big smile on her face.

"Patsy, we have a problem," Cam said quickly.

"What? What's wrong?" Patsy asked, her smile fading.

"Aimee is deaf. I did several tests."

"Are you sure?"

He explained the test that he had performed, and then Patsy repeated the test with the same results. Then, Cam repeated the test again.

Patsy burst into sobs. One of her first thoughts was, How are we going to teach her the gospel?

Patsy's mind turned quickly to one of her only experiences with deaf children. When she was thirteen, just after her family moved from Utah to California, she and her sisters sang to the deaf children at the John Tracy Clinic as part of a Disney Show. As Patsy sang, she saw that the deaf kids had been seated in a group in front of the hearing family members, and she noticed how inattentive they were. As she realized that they could not hear the music she so much enjoyed, she felt sad.

She never thought that she would experience this heartache

first hand. After about twenty minutes of testing, Cam and Patsy walked into their bedroom and kneeled down by their bed.

Cam offered a short and earnest prayer to Heavenly Father: "We have no idea what to do. We need help; please show us the way and bring us to the people who can help us."

After about an hour more of testing and discussion, the Walkers accepted the fact that Aimee could not hear; they were in shock, but not in denial. They knew that life would never be the same again. Nothing in their family experience, either before or after that moment, changed their lives more than that discovery.

They started to make calls. In tears, Patsy called her mom, and her mom helped her to calm down. Cam called his father, the doctor, who advised them calmly and said that he would call Dr. John House of the House Ear Institute and find out what he suggested.

With time, the Walkers began to make sense of some earlier experiences with Aimee.

For example, sometimes Patsy would enter a room where Aimee was lying on the bed fussing. She would clap and say, "Aimee," but Aimee would not react. Her heart would sink. Then, she would approach Aimee, sit on the bed, and look at her. Aimee would smile, and Patsy would think, She's fine.

On the fourth of July, when Aimee was four months old, the extended family had gathered to watch fireworks at Grace Park in Burbank. Patsy's mother noticed the reactions of the other kids and babies to the fireworks: hollers, screams, and cries. Aimee was unaffected.

Once at a PTA meeting, when Aimee was nine months old, in her baby seat but still unable to sit up, an older child had stood next to Aimee and shook some keys. Aimee didn't react.

In hindsight, the Walkers could see that Aimee had heard nothing in each situation.

Patsy took Aimee to Dr. Jay Gordon, her sister's doctor, who worked in Santa Monica. Using a tuning fork, Dr. Gordon determined that Aimee had a hearing problem and gave her the

Gazel developmental test.

"Aimee's delivery damaged her brain; just picture a tremendous blow to her head. How that is going to affect her for the rest of her life, we don't know yet," explained Dr. Gordon.

He believed that hearing aids would allow Aimee to hear and that the developmental delay would disappear with time. He didn't know for sure, but he thought that without the hearing aids, Aimee's development would be slowed. That made perfect sense to the Walkers.

He referred them to a pediatric neurologist, Andrea Morrison, in Tarzana. He also referred them to the House Ear Institute for a professional hearing test.

Just before Thanksgiving, the Walkers took Aimee in for a brain stem hearing test at the Audiological Department of the House Ear Institute. The doctors anesthetized Aimee, placed earphones on her, and connected wires to different areas of her head. A screen displayed sounds that the brain detected. Throughout the test, the screen showed nothing. One doctor said, "That doesn't mean that she has no hearing at all. She may still have some sensitivity to low vibra-tactile stimulation."

After multiple hearing tests, they worked with the House Ear Institute to try to get hearing aids. Betty Peterson, head audiologist for House Ear Institute, gave Aimee several audiograms and then said, "Your daughter may have a slight hearing problem, but that is not her main problem. Her main problem is that her brain is not sending a message to her ears. She is hearing things, but her central nervous system is so delayed or damaged that there is no communication between the brain and ears."

Betty Peterson sent Patsy to an integration therapist, Mary Silverstein, who tested Aimee thoroughly, to see if she had an intellectual disability.

Mary explained the results to Patsy: "It's doubtful that Aimee will ever be able to learn sign language because she is not computing concepts." For example, Mary explained that "Aimee will see something like a vase, but she won't be able to connect that that vase is a vase. She won't be able to make meaning out of images and create language."

These findings threw Patsy into a depression. She felt
overwhelmed when she thought about what she was being told.

Still, Patsy felt that the specialists were not seeing the
brightness emanating from Aimee's eyes.

At ten-and-a-half months, Aimee got the hearing aids, and
Patsy had to put a hat on her with a scarf that tied under her chin
because she would pull them out. Patsy figured that Aimee's
long hair would cover the hearing aids from the view of others.

Audiologists at the House Ear Institute sent the Walkers to
the John Tracy Clinic, a demonstration school for parents to
learn how to raise oral deaf children. The Walkers drove to the
John Tracy Clinic four times a week, a requirement for entrance
into their demonstration preschool: two visits to Demo Home,
one visit to Friday Family School, and one visit to Instruction
and Group Therapy. The clinic became a second religion for the
Walkers.

Church and family members pulled back from the Walkers
because Cam and Patsy were grieving so much and were so busy.
Group therapy comforted them; they felt most at home where
others were going through the same things, having the same
feelings, and discussing the same issues. In the group therapy
session, the adults met together, sitting in a large circle with a
psychologist, Dale Atkins. The Walkers noticed that because of
Aimee's health problems, the group therapy session for adults
was one of the few times that they had together without Aimee.

During these sessions, the Walkers saw people in much worse
situations than their own. One man blamed his wife for their son
being deaf, so he beat her up; then he left her. She came to group
therapy wearing sunglasses to cover her black eye.

Another child had Treacher Collins Syndrome, a disease that
involves facial deformities. She had no ears, along with a host of
other problems.

Although most people at the therapy sessions could relate
to each other, many of the couples divorced over the challenges
with their children. Usually, the mothers attended the sessions;

the fathers had already left because they couldn't handle the problems. Those who attended the therapy sessions became friends. They knew each other's pain and suffering, and they could talk to each other.

The clinic considered parents and professionals as equals in teaching the kids, and they taught parents to play the matching game with their deaf children. Patsy spent almost every minute of every day playing the matching game. She would pick something up that made sound and shake it, getting Aimee to look at Patsy's mouth. She would shake the item again and say, "I hear that," trying to help Aimee understand what sound was because she didn't understand that her voice made sound. They also worked with a phonador, a microphone connected to a metal rod that vibrated in Aimee's hand when she made sound. Patsy would try to get Aimee to make a sound by demonstrating: "Ba, ba, ba, ba, ba." Patsy also would hum with her mouth on Aimee's arm and place Aimee's hand on Patsy's throat. And she had another tool: a stuffed dog whose eyes would light up when sound was made. They used various vibra-tactile means to try to teach Aimee that her voice made sound.

As Cam and Patsy reflected on Aimee's situation, they couldn't reconcile Aimee's baby blessing with her health problems. How could Aimee be "a light to the world" and "touch others" as promised in her blessing if she didn't have a voice?

3 How Could Things Get Any Worse?

After one stressful day at work, Cam came home and said, "I want to go play basketball." Aimee was a year and a half and ill, and Jamie was four and had a fever. Danny was nine and the only healthy one.

"Don't go," Pasty said.

"Pats, I'm only going to play one game, maybe two at the most," Cam said.

"I don't have a good feeling about this," Patsy said. Cam left to play basketball at the park. Cam felt that he needed a break from the stress and strain of all the problems. Patsy wanted to kill him; she felt as if he had abandoned them.

Patsy said, "Danny, watch Aimee," and she helped Jamie into some tepid bath water to cool him off and then called Dr. Gordon, their family doctor, for advice. Suddenly, Jamie plunged face down in the water, as a grand mal seizure began, and Patsy saw air bubbles rising around Jamie's face. Patsy grabbed him, holding the phone between her ear and shoulder, crying and pleading on the phone to Dr. Gordon, "Oh, my gosh, he has gone into a convulsion. What do I do? I think he stopped breathing."

Danny knew just what he could do because he had done it twice before when Jamie had suffered a seizure: He ran to the neighbor's house to call the paramedics—since Patsy was using their only phone.

Dr. Gordon told Patsy, "Calm down. Just calm down. He is going to be okay. He has been through this before. Just stay there." Dr. Gordon continued, "Lean his head back slightly, pinch his nose closed with your fingers, blow into his mouth, release, blow into his mouth again, release, and so on." She repeated this six or seven times.

Jamie continued to convulse, eyes rolled back in his head, back arched, frothing at the mouth. Patsy tried to dry him off with a towel. She kissed his forehead and prayed out loud: "Please, dear God, let him be okay. Please, please, I beg of you, let my Jamie be okay." Patsy repeated this simple prayer countless times. She called her mother and asked her to get someone over to the park and tell Cam what had happened.

The paramedics put Jamie in the ambulance and headed for the hospital with Patsy, just as Cam was returning from the park to watch Danny and Aimee. Patsy prayed all the way to the hospital, begging Father in Heaven to let him be okay. The paramedics had strapped Jamie down in the bed and turned on their siren only as they crossed intersections. Cam met them at Children's Hospital later. The doctors suspected that Jamie had diabetes, but tests proved negative. Patsy received a calm feeling that everything was going to be fine. Jamie emerged from the seizure completely exhausted, drained of energy, and unable to communicate for some time, but, otherwise, okay.

Later, Cam and Patsy sat in Dr. Morrison's waiting room as the nurse prepared Jamie and Aimee for the EEG that the doctor had ordered because of all their health problems. Patsy thought, How is it possible that two of our children would require such an extreme test? Aimee had already gone through so many tests, including a CAT scan. After reviewing the results, Dr. Morrison told the Walkers that Aimee had a thin skull, the type of which is seen in very old people, but there was no calcification—a good sign. The doctor explained that Aimee was not in the normal range but believed that she would one day develop her motor skills and be able to walk. But it would be late, perhaps at the age of four or five. The doctor then said, "There's one test that you have not done yet: vision. I'd like you to go to Dr. Roger Friedman to have her eyes checked."

When they took Aimee to see Dr. Friedman, he looked at Aimee's eyes—saying nothing—and put drops in them. Then he said, "Okay, let her play and come back in twenty minutes." When they came back, Patsy held Aimee, who looked into a screen while doctor Friedman looked into Aimee's eyes. Dr. Friedman again said nothing during the exam; as he finished the eye exam, he directed the Walkers to sit back on the couch. He spoke to himself into a voice recorder: "Child has coloboma in right eye." He continued with a few other medical terms and said, "Patching the left eye to strengthen the right eye would be like beating a dead horse." He then looked at Patsy like she was supposed to understand.

"What do you mean," Patsy said, "beating a dead horse and patching? Is there a problem?"

"Yes, she has a coloboma, and the central retina tissue either didn't form or was destroyed by the lack of oxygen during the delivery."

"What does that mean?"

He said, "She is basically blind in her right eye. She will detect some light and dark and some peripheral shadows."

Patsy said, "Are you sure? I have a hard time believing that."

"You're welcome to get a second opinion," he responded, "but this is my finding."

"Okay, thank you very much . . . quack!" Patsy said—inaudibly. She and Cam left the office devastated. In the moments when Patsy allowed herself to believe it, she felt as though she had been shot in the heart.

With Jamie's seizures and Aimee's health problems, Cam and Patsy's lives had changed dramatically.

Patsy had never pictured herself going through anything like this. "This doesn't fit in my life," she said to herself. Patsy's sisters and family grew up singing. They had planned to travel and sing and perform as adults—their life mission. They performed at firesides and temple programs in various states, wrote music, recorded music, signed record contracts, appeared on television, and sang in movies.

The Walkers used to have a rich social life with a circle of good friends with whom they would take turns having a gourmet dinner at one couple's home each month. They also used to enjoy young married couple's activities, like game night with Mormon Trivia, Trivial Pursuit, Hearts, Rook, Pit, or Monopoly. They also loved playing tennis.

But their new reality supplanted the old one.

While their friends in and out of the church went on with their predictable lives, the Walkers' lives became increasingly complicated and consumed with the weight of their children's health problems. Between the ages of nine months and two and a half years, Aimee visited doctors or therapists five days a week: the House Ear Institute, the John Tracy Clinic, the Infant Stimulation Program for Cerebral Palsy, and the Loman School for Physical Therapy. To obtain services from each organization required a mound of paperwork and a battery of tests; visits to these clinics usurped at least four to six hours per day of Patsy's time. Before Aimee's birth, Patsy used to walk everywhere and feared driving on the freeways; all that changed when Patsy had to start taking Aimee to all of her appointments, which included driving in horrific traffic in downtown Los Angeles.

The challenges the Walkers faced caused sadness and a long period of grieving.

They then felt guilty about grieving because they had been taught that they should feel thankful and have a positive outlook.

The Walkers played the Glad Game, from *Pollyanna*, in which they hunted for the silver lining in negative situations. With time, the game became harder and harder to play. Cam served as a counselor in the bishopric, a leadership position in the church, and Patsy served as the Laurel Advisor, a leadership position in the young women's program. Both positions added stress to their lives. Their financial stress and children's health problems left them feeling like they were trapped in a dark hole—too many responsibilities and problems to negotiate.

They wanted some way to turn the situation around—into a blessing—but they didn't know how to do that.

Aimee kept receiving priesthood blessings in an attempt to solve her health problems. Patsy kept waiting and waiting for someone to bless Aimee with the ability to hear and see clearly, but she noticed that no priesthood holder ever said anything about restoring Aimee's senses.

The situation stressed the Walkers' marital relationship. They never considered divorce because they understood the significance of their temple marriage and what was in the best interest of their children, but their trials strained them to the limit. One conflict involved how to solve the problems they faced. Cam wanted to attend fewer meetings at the John Tracy Clinic; Patsy wanted to attend more meetings there. When they would go out to dinner or for a walk, they would discuss only Aimee's situation. Patsy obsessed about discussing it, and Cam wanted to talk about something else. In fact, he stopped attending group therapy.

Patsy, on the other hand, didn't want to attend an American Sign Language class because she couldn't picture herself signing in public and because of what she had been taught at the John Tracy Clinic: "Don't you dare teach your children sign language. If they learn to sign, they'll never learn to speak, and English is their God-given language."

Deaf panelists would come to group therapy sessions at the John Tracy Clinic and promote oral language, and some famous deaf people would come occasionally, like Lou Ferrigno and Jeff Float. These guests showed that learning to speak was possible, but the militant promotion of oralism over sign language at the John Tracy Clinic played into historical stereotypes undermining the validity of American Sign Language.

Historically, American Sign Language has been considered taboo. Deaf kids used to be sent away to schools to learn to become oral. If you wanted to sign, you had to do it in the back room. In public, it wasn't accepted. Patsy knew that people had taught sign language even to chimpanzees, and her daughter was not an animal.

Although Patsy believed the God-given-right argument, she had a few experiences that called it into question. She met some panelists from the John Tracy Clinic in other settings who would advocate American Sign Language by saying how sad they were growing up as deaf people in a hearing world and what an unbelievable release they felt when they finally learned American Sign Language, which typically happened later in life. They explained that their parents had not learned to sign and one deaf person said, "It's so hard. Our language is American Sign Language, and they were never willing to learn it. Don't make that mistake with your child."

A young mother who also had a deaf child at the John Tracy Clinic gave Patsy *Deaf Like Me*, a book in which the author, Tom Spradley, chronicled how Louise, his wife, contracted German measles during her pregnancy, resulting in a deaf daughter, Lynn. In the process of raising Lynn, the Spradleys traveled to California to attend the John Tracy Clinic and found themselves in the middle of the oral/manual debate. After failing to make progress through years of training in lip-reading, Lynn began to learn American Sign Language; her first signs included "I love you." At the beginning, Lynn could make the signs but did not understand their meaning; with coaching, the moment of understanding finally came like the moment that Helen Keller understood that the word that Anne Sullivan was spelling in her hand, w-a-t-e-r, named the liquid flowing over her hands. This understanding animated and motivated Lynn to crave more signs; she learned a symbol for herself, her name, which validated her existence, and the names of things around her. After learning to sign, Lynn's communication replaced her tantrums.

Lynn's story profoundly influenced Patsy's perspective.

Something else at the John Tracy Clinic altered Patsy's thinking. Some of the adults pulled and slapped the kids' hands when they pointed, saying, "No, you have to talk. Use your voice." A few adults went so far as to put a piece of paper in front of their mouths while talking to the kids to try to develop and use some residual hearing. The children tried to guess what the adults were saying. The kids would run away and put their hands over their eyes. Patsy was having a hard time picturing Aimee in this environment.

Also, by turning the TV on with the volume off, Patsy could see how difficult lip-reading was.

Cam bought in to American Sign Language from the beginning, had attended a night class for about three months at North Hollywood High Adult School, had learned about 300 signs, and felt excited about it. Patsy had attended only a couple of times, and one night she decided to attend again although she still felt that learning American Sign Language was a mistake. She sat behind her husband in class, which Ms. Pearmutter taught, an interpreter from the California State University at Northridge, who was thin with a plain appearance, thick glasses, and dishwater blond hair. She typically wore pants and t-shirts. She was the most beautiful and inspirational signer imaginable—full of passion for signing and people with disabilities; her boyfriend was blind. The room was a regular high school classroom with rows of desks, and she taught about Deaf culture as well. She used neither books nor handouts. The class, American Sign Language 1, consisted of 25-30 students, mostly adults, including Patsy's mom and brother, three sisters—members of the Clinger family—and Cam. The thought of being able to communicate with Aimee motivated the Clingers to attend, except for Patsy, who attended that Tuesday night grudgingly.

That evening, Ms. Pearmutter explained, "Only one or two deaf people in a thousand will become really proficient at lip-reading, and those two individuals will understand only about 50% of a conversation." This sentence cut Patsy to the quick and contradicted everything that she was learning at the John Tracy Clinic. Patsy thought, Oh, my gosh, what do we do?

Patsy started feeling tingly and couldn't breathe. She tapped Cam on the shoulder and whispered, "Something's happening." Then she went numb and passed out. Cam carried her out and drove her to the emergency room. When she regained consciousness, she recalled eating some cookies at a fundraiser prior to attending the American Sign Language class, and she thought that someone had tried to poison her and felt that she was dying.

The doctors said that Patsy had an extreme anxiety attack and hyperventilated.

After going to many doctors and taking a series of tests to determine the problem, including a five-hour glucose-tolerance test, Patsy learned that she had developed a severe case of hypoglycemia. Her blood sugar would drop, and she couldn't raise it. Her resting heart rate was 130-150. From having babies and miscarriages, she also had pernicious anemia, which required Cam to administer a weekly shot. She dropped down to 92 pounds.

After passing out in class, Patsy started panicking on a daily basis.

At her lowest point, she sat in the living room, and she felt an attack coming. She felt as if she was going numb, her mouth started watering, and her body started shaking. She felt like she had to get to the bathroom to vomit; she also had diarrhea. Too weak to walk, she crawled into the bathroom, pulled herself up onto the toilet, and thought, I am dying. I really am dying. Who is going to raise my children? She had lost control of her health and her mind. She wouldn't look into the mirror because she could see the fear in her own face, which scared her to death. She felt as if someone had a hold of her heart, like someone had a knee on her chest. When she couldn't get a deep breath, she started breathing into a brown lunch bag.

Through reflection, Patsy eventually realized the cause of her breakdown: she felt guilty about Aimee's health problems when most of them could have been avoided through a C-section.

Both Cam and Patsy understood that Patsy might become an invalid—or die.

In fact, Patsy told Cam, "I think that you should have a vasectomy because I don't think that I could survive having another child."

Cam said, "Well, you know, Patsy, if you die, I would want to have more children."

Cam thought that the conversation was insignificant in their relationship.

Patsy thought, How could things get any worse?

4 Look Bird Tree

Patsy sat with her three children in church in the Studio City Ward, her local congregation in North Hollywood. Cam sat on the stand next to Bishop Doty. Three of her sisters and their families who also lived in the ward surrounded Patsy in the middle of the center section.

A young married woman, thin and tall, with strawberry-blond hair and freckles, stood at the pulpit. She wore a dark, feminine suit and glasses, and she spoke with a slight Utah accent: "I have been asked to speak on how we can build our faith." Shortly after she gave the title of her talk, she boldly said, "God does not give fear power. God gives faith power." She spoke clearly and emphatically and distinctly, but not dramatically: "If you have fear, you cannot have faith."

Patsy thought, You are right. I can and will overcome my fear. As Patsy realized that she needed to replace fear with faith, she began to feel better.

Patsy had been very healthy up to this point in her life. Even when everyone in the house had the flu and she started to get it, she could talk herself out of it, but when she had so much control over her health, she lacked empathy for others. After her breakdown, she realized that people who have fears or chronic illnesses and can't overcome them deserve her patience. Patsy's panic attacks prepared her to empathize with others who suffered and to love others more deeply. She understood how important a caring husband, a loving family, a thoughtful doctor, friends, blessings, and support are.

She could also see that she needed to experience trials to acquire this patience, understanding, and compassion for other people. She became thankful for her problems—horrible experiences, but useful in her progression.

A series of steppingstones combined to bolster this shift in Patsy's perspective and create a turning point for the Walkers.

At Children's Hospital of Los Angeles, she sat in a big chair with Aimee on her lap, anticipating a second opinion about Aimee's vision. The doctor checked Aimee and said, "I've got some great news," confirming their conviction that the first ophthalmologist was a quack. "In eighty-five percent of these cases, the problem is bilateral."

"Bilateral?"

"Meaning both eyes," he explained. "And she only has it in one. Can you believe it? She has one good eye." The doctor's positive outlook was contagious. The Walkers danced out of the office thinking, Thank you, God. Our daughter has one good eye.

Also, Patsy's doctor, Dr. Judd Goodman, moved his practice to New York about the time of Aimee's birth but kept in touch with his replacement in California, through whom he received updates about Aimee's array of health problems. When Aimee was about a year old, Dr. Goodman finally called Patsy directly and said, "I want you to know that I did everything properly. I really feel as if I did what was right in every way. I considered your health and the baby's health equally, but I want you to know that I have malpractice insurance, and it's for situations like this. If you feel that you should sue me to get the proper care for your daughter, I want you to do that. We want your daughter's quality of life to be the best that it can be."

Because the Walkers wanted the best treatment for Aimee, they discussed the offer, thought about it, and prayed about it.

The doctor, Patsy, and Cam as a team had decided not to deliver Aimee through a C-section, but the doctor had led in that decision, which protected Patsy at Aimee's expense. Patsy still felt guilty about not opposing the doctor's position because anoxia is a contributor to deafness, blindness, and neurological problems. Maybe the hip sheath would have been her only problem; Aimee could have grown up in a way that any normal, beautiful young woman would have.

The Walkers finally realized that a lawsuit would involve years of litigation, and suing others was incongruent with their values. They felt that somehow everything was going to be okay, and they declined Dr. Goodman's invitation.

Dr. Goodman's call began to lift a burden off of Patsy's shoulders. His words comforted her, but the guilt would not dissipate entirely for four years.

Another time, Dessin Meyer, a member of the ward, came up to Patsy at church and said, "What is really wrong with Aimee? Come sit down. Let's talk about it." Patsy welcomed the invitation to talk. Most people treated Patsy and Aimee as if they had a disease: don't get too close or you'll catch it. Aimee had a brace and a body aid—a brown vest with a pocket on the chest that held an amplification device from which wires ran to Aimee's ears; people didn't know what to think and kept their distance. Patsy felt such a relief about being able to talk about it, let down her guard, and set aside her fears. She appreciated his compassion.

When Aimee was a year and a half old, the LA Unified School District sent Eileen Obrien of the Infant Stimulation Program to the Walkers on a weekly basis for a year. After setting up an Individualized Education Program, Eileen promoted American Sign Language with the Walkers. She would bring little books and teach very basic signs, which Patsy still resisted because she had Aimee on the waitlist for the John Tracy Clinic Preschool where

Aimee was going to learn to speak. Eileen explained what the John Tracy Clinic had not: if children don't develop a language by the age of three—English, American Sign Language, or any other language—they can't develop cognitively at a normal rate. This news shook Patsy to the core. After she learned that, she opened her mind up to learning signs.

Eileen brought with her hope. She worked with some other profoundly disabled children, and she would proudly note Aimee's weekly progress. Aimee's first signs were "food" and "bottle."

At a year and a half, Aimee would move her mouth because she saw her parents talking, and she wanted to be like them, but she didn't make any sound when she moved her mouth. They had been using the phonader and the mechanical dog whose eyes would light up. The Walkers also had a ring that suctioned to the wall of the bathtub to help Aimee sit up. One day as Aimee sat in the bathtub next to Jamie, Patsy took Aimee's hand and placed it on her mouth, saying, "Ma, ma, ma, ma" to try to get Aimee to understand that the mouth made sound. Aimee didn't understand what the mouth could do: she couldn't blow out a candle despite practice, and her kisses lacked suction. Then, Patsy would place her own hand on Aimee's mouth, encouraging Aimee to copy Patsy and produce sound. They would go back and forth.

Suddenly, Aimee got it. She started making sound through her mouth, and she realized that she made sound. She knew she had a voice. This is what they had been working toward— throughout each day for eight months. Patsy called Maura at the John Tracy Clinic and announced, "You won't believe it. Aimee put it together. She knows her mouth makes sound." This was a small, but significant step. The value lay in Aimee's realization that she had a voice; that understanding empowered her. It was more powerful than the limited use of her voice.

When Aimee was about two years and eight months, she was sitting on Patsy's lap as she sat on a step in the backyard of their home on Hartsook. Patsy wore a sweatshirt, blue jeans, and cowboy boots; Aimee wore a pastel play dress with black leggings. Grass grew right up to the cement patio and around the guava bush; various trees of different sizes lined the fence at the back of the yard. Patsy supported Aimee with her left hand and slowly signed one word at a time to Aimee with her right hand: sky, blue, tree, and so on.

Then a brown bird the size of a small dove flew into one of the trees along the fence and perched on a branch, looking toward Aimee and Patsy, clearly visible between the large, dark leaves.

Aimee pointed up and signed, "Look bird tree."

Patsy started crying. Aimee had put together a full sentence, a complete thought. Patsy was so thrilled that she got on the phone and called everyone that she knew, starting with her mother. Patsy could not have been more proud had Aimee won the Nobel Peace Prize. It was like a hearing child uttering a sentence for the first time: "Look, there is a bird in the tree." Melody, Patsy's older sister who had always believed that Aimee was exceptional, said, "I told you—she's brilliant. You can see the light in her eyes." On an earlier occasion, Melody had said, "When Aimee looks into my eyes, it's like she is looking right into my soul."

Patsy knew from that point on that Aimee would be able to communicate, that she would be bright, and that she would make out okay in life. Patsy thought, If Aimee can see what happened, understand it, feel joy at seeing the bird, communicate it, and put all that together, she will be just fine. This was a profound moment in Patsy's life in regard to Aimee's well being.

Patsy recalled the olive analogy that they used so often at the John Tracy Clinic. Getting the first olive out of the bottle is the hardest, but the olives do flow after that first one comes. This doesn't just apply to oral language; it applies to all language, including American Sign Language. Aimee had found her voice—not an auditory voice, but a voice nonetheless, one that could be translated into English or any other language. Patsy began to appreciate American Sign Language as a beautiful, complex, in-depth language that can communicate any idea. She had at first thought that if animals can be taught signs, how complex could American Sign Language be? But with time, she grew to understand its nature as a visual language, a complete language in its own right.

Patsy learned about some research that indicated that in families with hearing children who are taught American Sign Language before they can speak, those children do better academically than children in hearing families who are not introduced to American Sign Language. Also, sign language is easier to learn than oral language.

Some deaf people of the past generation who learned American Sign Language when it was socially unacceptable only learned to express simple ideas in basic ways; society robbed them of the opportunity to learn the complexities, intricacies, and depth of the language.

By the time that Aimee reached the age of three, Patsy was sold on the importance of learning American Sign Language, but she still had dreams of Aimee speaking, and the Walkers continued to pay for speech therapy.

One evening, the Walkers went out to dinner on a date night and overheard a conversation by another couple about someone named Rusty and how much he loved to play with a ball. Listening to the conversation helped them to take their minds off of their problems. Then they realized that the couple was talking about their dog, and that they probably didn't even have any kids. Cam and Patsy realized how fortunate they were to have three wonderful children. They understood that they had problems, but they thought about the progress that they had made and how the college of life was granting them an education on deafness and schooling them in how to develop Christ-like attributes. They decided to take a positive approach, saying, "We're going to embrace this new world we've been given and make the best out of it. We're going to make a difference."

Another experience showed the Walkers something positive about Aimee. Eddy Racine lived in North Hollywood too. At

6'2" and almost 400 pounds, he was broad, and he carried scars from an earlier accident.

Many years before the Walkers met Eddy, Eddy and some friends had gathered to celebrate New Year's Eve when he was a senior at Corona High School in Norco. To start a fire, Eddy had turned on the gas and reached into the fireplace with a match to light a gas log. The fireplace had been leaking gas, but Eddy could not detect it because the gas used in those days didn't have an odor. The gas in the fireplace exploded into a fireball, burning Eddy from the waist up, including his arms, chest, and face. Doctors did not expect him to live; he spent six months in the hospital and lost part of his left ear. He had a fish-shaped mouth and horrendous scarring on his face, which made him look mean.

Long after Eddy's recovery, he and Cam grew close as they served together in the church. For a while, Cam served as the stake young men's president, a leadership position over the young men in North Hollywood, while Eddy's boys participated in the program.

Eddy had trouble finding work because his appearance scared people. Cam asked Rocky Cohen, a Jewish friend of the family, if he could get Eddy a job at Pepo Florists as a delivery man. After a week or two, Rocky called Cam to explain that he had to let Eddy go because he was scaring some of the customers to whom he was delivering flowers.

The Walkers treated Eddy like part of the family. They saw a wonderful person beneath the scars, but they also noticed how others reacted to him, the same way that people reacted to children with disabilities. The Walkers learned the importance of bending down to look into people's eyes and talking to them instead of to their caregivers.

Despite his hardships, Eddy increased in kindness and gratitude with each trial, and he sensed that the Walkers never judged him for his looks.

One Sunday, Patsy sat in church holding Aimee in her arms. Eddy came up to Patsy, kneeled down, and said, "Oh, Aimee is so pretty." Aimee reached her hand up to Eddy's face and softly touched all that hideous scarring. "You don't know how good that feels," he said, tears welling up in his eyes. "I am so scary to people—let alone children—and for her to feel my face and not be afraid. . . ."

Seeing Eddy's tears, Aimee made the sign for "pain" or "hurt," two index fingers tapping each other, with a questioning look on her face. Eddy asked Patsy what the sign meant. "Are you hurt or sad?" Patsy explained.

"No, I'm happy," Eddy replied, which Patsy communicated to Aimee.

Aimee made the sign for "hurt" or "pain" again, which Patsy translated again.

"No, I'm fine," Eddy said, giving Aimee a big hug.

From that time on, Eddy and Aimee had a bond. Eddy felt a kinship with Aimee. Any time that they saw each other, they both lit up.

After that experience, the Walkers understood that Aimee could speak to people's hearts and that she had an inner feeling for others and for their struggles. Instead of being put off by Eddy, she was drawn to him.

Eddy later told Cam, "Your daughter is so special because she touched my face without fear and asked me honest questions, and no one has ever done that to me before." Eddy added, "She and I have a special relationship." He wore that statement like a medal of honor.

As Patsy saw Aimee's influence on Eddy, she recalled Cam's words in Aimee's baby blessing: "You will be a light to the world, kind and loving, . . . and have a special compassion that will draw others to you and allow you to touch others."

Patsy and Cam began to understand that Aimee had a mission to fulfill.

5 Musical Chairs

When Aimee was four, Patsy drove Aimee home from school one day, and Ester Mathews, one of the neighbors from across the street, saw Patsy and walked over. Short, with salt and pepper hair, large glasses, a little heavy, and in her early 70s, Ester had brought coins in a bag for the kids for Hanukkah. The Walkers had joined the Mathews for Passover in the past, and they referred to her endearingly as "the mayor of the street" because she kept an eye on the events in the neighborhood and always warned people about certain situations. The Mathews were well loved.

As Ester walked over, Patsy got out of the blue Civic while Aimee sat in the passenger seat. While Ester and Patsy visited, Patsy heard a "click" and realized that Aimee had locked the car doors from the inside. The car was off, but the keys were still in the ignition.

Patsy started signing, "Aimee, Aimee! Open up." Aimee wore a flowered t-shirt with ruffled trim, hot pink leggings, white-laced socks, and black China shoes. Aimee just smiled like a little devil, climbed into the driver's seat, and turned the key. Because the car had a stick shift, it lurched forward spasmodically, advancing slowly down the long driveway. On her knees and embracing the huge steering wheel like Captain Hook, Aimee peered through the bottom of the windshield in delight.

"Cam, do something," Ester started yelling—so confused that she referred to Patsy as Cam. "Cam, do something!"

"Stop, Aimee, stop! You're going to hit the tree," Patsy signed and yelled. "You're going to crash the car. Stop!" Aimee kept smiling at Patsy from behind the wheel.

Frantic, Patsy remembered that their car had a sunroof, which was opened a crack, so she sprinted to the house, turned on the hose, and doused the little maniac from the sky, screaming, "Now, you stop it!"

Dripping wet, Aimee finally started signing "sorry, sorry," and Patsy got her to open the door after the car had veered off the driveway about ten feet.

Patsy simultaneously wanted to spank her and hug her, saying, "Never, never, never do that again!" Patsy grabbed Aimee's arm and walked her to her room, saying, "Go in your room and sit down and think about that. You come out and tell me when you're ready."

The experience demonstrated one of Aimee's traits: stubbornness, which has turned out to be both a curse and a blessing, and one reason for her success. She never gives up.

Aimee's first experience behind the wheel only played into Patsy's fears, which continued to worry Patsy in her dreams. When Aimee was young, Patsy had the same dream three times. In it, she was vacuuming the house. Then she heard a voice, but she knew that no one was home, except for Aimee. From the bedroom, Patsy heard Aimee talking to her dolls and singing "Twinkle, Twinkle, Little Star." Patsy thought, She could hear all this time; she has just been playing with us. Patsy turned the vacuum off and ran into the bedroom, saying "Aimee, Aimee, was that you? You can talk?" Then Aimee looked up at Patsy, unable to hear or speak a word, and then Patsy woke up.

Patsy had another dream after Aimee started walking. In the dream, Aimee would wander off at night, and Patsy knew that calling for her was pointless. She would search frantically for her everywhere. Then, finally, she would find Aimee, and she would wake up. She was so paranoid that Aimee would get away that she had Cam put up an eight-foot wrought iron fence around the pool. Around the yard, where the dirt didn't meet the bottom of the fence, Cam placed boards so that Aimee couldn't slip under the fence. He also had a gate installed to seal off the driveway. This dream of Patsy searching for Aimee reoccurred a dozen times when Aimee was young and continued on periodically until she was about seventeen or eighteen. This fear was well grounded because Aimee could not hear cars approaching and was particularly vulnerable on her right side, her blind side. Once, a drunk driver narrowly missed striking her at fifty miles per hour.

Patsy's greatest fear took form in the old movie *Johnny Belinda*, about a deaf girl who is raped. After all, Aimee was cute and vulnerable.

Aimee's teachers encouraged Patsy to send Aimee to school on the bus, saying this promoted Aimee's independence. All of the other kids took the bus. Aimee wanted to follow suit, and Patsy let her go despite her reservations. The bus driver was a big guy, about six feet tall, 250 pounds, and twenty-five years old. His route involved picking up only four kids for school, and Aimee was the first one he would pick up in the morning and the last one he would drop off in the afternoon, leaving the two of them alone in the bus. He often arrived late—once, an hour and a half late. Patsy didn't trust the bus driver, so one day she drove behind the bus undetected until she verified that Aimee was dropped off at school. Then he started making some questionable comments to Patsy: "Boy, you sure look pretty today. Those pants look great on you." Patsy thought, I don't trust this guy. He should not be driving little children. Then, Patsy noticed the bus driver once left the kids alone. That was the last straw. She started driving Aimee to school herself. Parent complaints eventually pressured the district into replacing the bus driver; his replacement was female, so Patsy sent Aimee to school on the bus again. Occasionally, the same male bus driver would drive as a substitute, and when he showed up, Patsy would make up an excuse: "Aimee won't be able to take the bus today because we will be dropping by grandma's house on the way to pick something up." Later, the male bus driver was fired for "inappropriate behavior." Patsy felt like she was always standing vigil.

Captain Jack, a man in his seventies, volunteered at the school, and after Patsy learned to communicate well with Aimee, she would warn Aimee: "You are not to go anywhere with Captain Jack or any other man unless your teacher goes with you. Some men want to do things that are not right."

As challenges increased for the Walkers, those around them took notice and assisted. Many mornings, the Walkers would open their front door and find gifts on the porch: a basket of baked breads, a turkey, a jar of fresh squeezed orange juice, or cookies. Once, someone left a set of clothes for each member of the family, including kids' clothing, a tweed suit for Patsy, and a pair of red Nike high-tops for Cam to play basketball in. An attached note said, "From the good fairy." Another note said, "We know you'll get through this. We love you." At Patsy's lowest point, a paid house cleaner appeared twice per month for three months.

One Sunday, Patsy walked up to the pulpit at church and said, "I just want to thank whoever is leaving gifts at our home." She cried. These gifts sustained the Walkers through their trials, but the memory of these gifts outlasted the gifts themselves and became even more valuable because of their power to sustain the family in subsequent trials.

With time, Aimee continued to develop, and her personality continued to emerge. In her Deaf and Hard of Hearing program at school, little girls would line up to have Aimee French-braid their hair. Aimee could see that many of the other girls didn't have the things that she had, so she would give away her own hair ribbons, hair clips, headbands, berets, bracelets, and rings. Often, she would take a bag of these items to school to distribute. Aimee also gave away one of her father's high school yearbooks, without asking either of her parents first, because she understood that some of the poor children in her class didn't have any books that special. Cam's mother had custom dolls made for each of her granddaughters, and Aimee gave her custom doll away to Rosie at school. Patsy said, "Why did you give your special doll away?"

"Rosie doesn't have one," Aimee said. "It's fine. I have another doll."

Because of years in an infant stimulation program and physical therapy, Aimee started catching up to her peers physically—running around with her brothers and friends. The summer after kindergarten, Aimee played T-ball as her first sport, and she was both the only girl and the only deaf player on the Twins team. She wore a white bow in her hair, lacey socks, and goggles to protect her good eye. In "Magic Played Out on Field of Dreams," an article about Aimee that appeared in the *Daily News* on August 23, 1989, D.G. Fulford wrote that Aimee "is tiny and as delicate as a dragonfly." Cam coached the team, and Aimee's brother, Jamie, who also played on the team, did most of the interpreting for Aimee. As number twenty-seven, she played center field, and she would chase all the balls that came into the outfield, including right and left field. Sometimes she would even take the ball away from her own teammates. When it was her turn to bat, she would hit the ball on the T, and if it didn't go very far, she would run out and pick it up herself, place it back on the T, and hit it again.

Although the Twins never won a single game all season, something magical happened: all the kids learned the rules of the game, learned how to bring a high level of energy to the sport, and learned how to support each other as members of a team. They felt like champions. The Walkers also learned that Aimee was a social butterfly with the ability to inspire others.

When Aimee was young, Cam introduced silent mealtime

to help the family learn to sign, to avoid leaving Aimee out of communication. They did this as often as they could when meals weren't rushed. He would say, "Only sign." The kids learned American Sign Language faster than the adults. One morning, Jamie sat down at the table for some cereal, and Cam pulled the bowl back and said, "No, you have to sign something to eat."

"What? I'm hungry," Jamie said.

"Sign it, and I'll give it to you," Cam said.

"Come on, Dad," Jamie said. Aimee sneaked into the dining room where Jamie could see her, but out of Cam's sight, and signed, "Please, Dad," which Jamie signed to Cam.

Cam signed, "Fine," turning into the dining room. "But don't tell him next time, Aimee."

Many times, Aimee had to clandestinely provide signs to Danny and Jamie so they could eat with the family. Although Cam was so busy with heavy work and church responsibilities, he never lost sight of the importance of including Aimee in dinner conversation.

One time when she was about six years old, Aimee was playing with her cousins, and she and her cousin, Melissa, both wanted the same toy. Melissa was holding the toy, and Aimee grabbed it, signing, "That's mine."

"No, that's mine," Melissa responded, ripping it away from Aimee and freaking out. She got so mad that she grabbed Aimee's head and pulled out a chunk of hair the size of a quarter.

Both girls looked at the tuft of hair hanging limply in Melissa's hand—trying to register what had happened. Melissa tried to run away, but, Aimee, motivated by the pain in her scalp, dropped the toy, overtook Melissa, and scratched her in the face like a cat, catching some skin beneath her fingernails.

Melissa ran to her mother, her face scratched deeply.

A few minutes later, the mothers brought the girls together to apologize. "I'm sorry," each girl confessed.

Melissa's mom, Leesa, said, "Okay, now give Aimee her hair back" because she was still holding on to it. She wouldn't let go of it.

Finally, she handed the hair back to Aimee, who looked at Patsy, signing, "Mom, can you glue it to my head?"

Patsy died laughing, and Leesa broke into laughter too.

Heather, another cousin who was always a peacemaker, said to Aimee, "Don't worry. Your hair 'll grow back. Poor Melissa, she is probably going to have a scar."

Aimee felt horrible and apologized repeatedly throughout the day: "I'm sorry. Forgive me, please." Then she tried to give all of her toys to Melissa. "Here, you can take everything home with you," Aimee said.

"I don't want your things. I don't want a scar!" Melissa replied.

"Don't worry," Heather said. "Thank goodness you'll wear makeup when you get older, and that'll cover it all up."

Aimee had to wear her hair in a ponytail to cover the bald spot until the hair grew back, but the scar on Melissa's face from a single fingernail never disappeared, even with makeup.

Now, when Aimee and Melissa get together, Aimee says, "I can't believe you ripped my hair out."

"I can't believe you scratched my face," says Melissa, adding, "I can't believe you said, 'Mom, can you glue it to my head.'" And they both laugh and laugh.

In kindergarten, Aimee had her first boyfriend, Franky Martinez, another student from her Deaf and Hard of Hearing class. He had brown skin, brown eyes, and black hair in a crew cut. He was taller than Aimee, like everyone else in the class. Aimee and more than a dozen of the other deaf kids in their class attended the party at his home in an apartment building. About half the parents came to the party, and they were all hearing parents. All the adults and kids were beginning signers, but the kids signed better than their parents.

For most of the kids, this was the first party they had attended outside of school, and they all wore cone-shaped hats attached under their chins with an elastic string. Enthralled in the joy of the moment, their facial expressions were animated, and they signed frequently, smiling and laughing beneath twisted streamers. The parents heard their unique laughter: loud, gleeful, atypical, and free from the restraint that comes from familiarity with the sound of one's own voice.

These deaf kids had grown up feeling disconnected. Many of their parents spoke Spanish, not English. The kids spoke neither language. Their laughter revealed how the isolation of deafness in the presence of other signers turns to delight.

They sang "Happy Birthday," the parents singing and signing while the kids signed, following the lead of Franky's mom. At the end of the song, they applauded, the kids shaking their open hands in the air.

They began to play games, beginning with Pop the Balloon. The kids sat in chairs arranged in a circle to play the game; Franky's mom passed out balloons of various colors and gave directions in English and simplified ASL. Each child tried to pop his or her balloon by sitting on it. Many of the balloons slid out from behind little rear ends, and the kids tried to pop them by stomping on them. With each popped balloon, the parents flinched; the kids did not. Instead, they felt the exuberance that only kindergarteners feel with such an accomplishment.

They also played musical chairs. The chairs in the circle were rotated to face out, and Franky's mother explained how the game would work: they would use no music. Instead, when the lights went on, the kids would circulate around the chairs. When the lights went off, everyone would search for an empty seat. She then closed the blinds. As the kids played the game, they fought for empty chairs, eliminating kids one by one until there remained only two chairs and three kids: Franky, Rachel, and Aimee, who always had a competitive edge. When the lights went out, Rachel was eliminated. Everyone was laughing, and then Franky and Aimee vied for one chair. The lights went out for the last time, and Franky just looked away and let Aimee sit in the chair. Aimee understood that that meant he liked her. Aimee signed, "Come on. Sit down with me. We'll share the chair and both be winners." Franky sat down and remained Aimee's hand-holding boyfriend until she transferred to Tripod, a new school, about a year later.

6 "It's Okay. It's All Right"

Aimee grew up playing basketball with her brothers on the garage hoop. She was short and fast, so she would steal the ball away from others. Aimee's father, Cam, served as assistant coach for the co-ed basketball team the first year that Aimee played at the age of six, and he developed a special play for each player. Aimee had the shoelace play in which Cam would sign to Aimee that it was time for her play, so she would know it was coming. Then, Aimee would untie her shoelace and continue to play until Cam would yell and sign, without calling a timeout, "Aimee, your shoe is untied. Come here. Tie your shoe." Aimee's teammates would dribble the ball away from her, and the defender guarding Aimee would drift away from her too. After Aimee had tied her lace, she quickly cut to the basket. Her teammate would then pass her the ball for an uncontested layup, which sometimes dropped in the basket.

Sometimes Aimee would forget to dribble during games. Cam would say, "You've got to remember to bounce the ball." Her strength was her defense; she was like a fly on her opponents, tenacious, but she fouled a lot in games because she was used to her brothers allowing her to hang on them when they played in the driveway. In games, if she couldn't stop the opponents, she would pull on their jerseys.

When Aimee would foul out of a game, Cam would call her out, and Aimee would say, "Me. Are you sure? I don't think so. No, no, I want to stay." Then, Cam would come over and explain. Aimee would then leave the court dejectedly.

With her one eye, catching the ball and shooting were challenges; however, one time, Aimee ran behind the three-point line with the ball and took a shot. The ball sailed through the air and swished into the net. Her teammates were so excited that they ran over to her and hugged her. Some people in the crowd came onto the floor to hug Aimee also. The referee had to blow the whistle to disperse everyone so that the game could go on. One of the boys on the team said, "Wow. I'm going to pass it to you. You make another one like that." At the end of the game, one of the boys passed the ball to Aimee, who took a short bank shot off the glass that went in to score the winning basket.

After Aimee's game, the family would watch Jamie's game, then Danny's game. After all the games, the whole family would stay in the gym playing horse until someone kicked them out.

While the Walkers were playing basketball, Aimee's cousins, Jessica, Melissa, and Rahny, were taking gymnastics classes at LA Valley College, and their mothers encouraged Patsy to sign Aimee up for gymnastics. Aimee kept bugging Patsy to call about gymnastics, so one day she did. She signed Aimee up on the phone, and just before the conversation ended, Patsy said, "By the way, Aimee is deaf. I hope that that's not going to be a problem."

The lady on the phone replied, "Oh, wow. We don't have a coach that can sign. We had one, but she is no longer working here. I'm sorry, but we are not going to be able to accommodate Aimee." Aimee had already gotten a little pink tutu for gymnastics at Christmas, and she was very upset about being rejected. Patsy was upset, and so was her sister, Debra.

A couple of days later, Debra called and said, "I've got some good news and some bad news."

"What's the good news?" Patsy asked.

"We can get Aimee into Valley College," said Debra.

"Really. How's that?" replied Patsy.

"Well, that's the bad news. Rahny broke her foot after just one class. We have paid for two months, and Aimee can take her spot. The woman in the office never goes into the gym, so Aimee can just take Rahny's place." Then, Debra added, "Just tell Aimee not to sign, to just do what the other kids are doing. A lot of the kids are quiet."

Patsy brought Aimee to her first gymnastics practice and said, "Remember. Don't sign. Just follow the other kids." Patsy stayed to watch the practice.

The kids practiced everything: floor, bars, vault, and beam. They walked on the beam, which was resting on the floor mat, and Aimee kept falling off because being deaf and blind in one eye affected her balance. The coach grabbed her hand and helped her control her wobbling.

After class, Aimee was just watching other kids practice, and the coach called her name, "Aimee. Aimee." Since Aimee didn't turn her head to look, the coach repeated herself: "Aimee, Aimee, pay attention."

One of the kids tapped Aimee and said, "Look at the coach," and Aimee turned to the coach and signed, "What?"

The coach, Dawn Salizar said, "I'm trying to tell you something."

Aimee's face turned white, and she looked at her mom and signed, "What did she say?"

Patsy signed to Aimee, "Darn, Aimee, you're not supposed to sign anything."

The coach said, "Is that sign language? You must be deaf." She walked over to Patsy and said, "Is your daughter deaf?"

"Yes, she is," Patsy admitted.

"I can't believe that. She learns so quickly. She really has a lot of skill." The coach thought for a moment. "I've got it. She can teach me sign language, and I can teach her gymnastics."

After just a few practices, Dawn said to Patsy, "If you can afford it, I want you to also put Aimee in my advanced class because she has jumped so far past the kids in the class that I don't want to hold her back." By the end of two months, Aimee was doing back hand springs and being spotted on layouts.

She was also attending open workouts where, one night, girls from Santa Monica Gymnastics Center noticed Aimee and said, "Wow, she has only been doing gymnastics for two months!"

Then, Zelda, the head of the parents' group, said to Patsy, "Please have her come try out at our gym. We know she'll get a scholarship."

By the end of the summer, Dawn insisted that Aimee participate in the Santa Monica Beach Meet, held outdoors on the sand in the cool afternoon sea breeze. Aimee had no United Sports Governing Foundation number and had no clue about competitions, but she looked cute in her white leotard that Grandma Clinger had adorned with red flowers and diamonds. Patsy double French-braided Aimee's hair and tied it off with red ribbons. Dawn selected the music for Aimee's floor routine: Disney's "Electric Light Parade."

Without fully understanding the requirements for the meet, how long the routine should be, or what her music sounded like, Aimee received a score of 7.6. People started saying to Patsy, "She has talent." Aimee felt as though she had wings in gymnastics, and she felt hungry to compete at a higher level.

The Walkers also learned that while Aimee was at a disadvantage in the hearing world in school and social settings, gymnastics provided a level playing field, a venue for showcasing her talents.

When Aimee was seven, the Walker family attended a regional conference church meeting. Aimee and a few other deaf people were sitting in front watching the interpreter. Aimee sat between her parents. The speaker was a mission president, and he was sharing what had happened to his grandmother many years ago. She was deaf and had been all of her life. She was not a member of the church, but the missionaries came to her house and taught her about Jesus Christ, the plan of salvation, and Joseph Smith. Although she was in her 90s, she learned quickly. She believed what she was taught, and the Spirit gave her an impression that she should be baptized and become a member of the Church. Because she lived in a rural area and it was winter, the church leaders had to cut a hole in the ice in a lake to baptize her. When she came out of the water, she could suddenly hear. It was a miracle.

Aimee looked over and tapped Mom and Dad and said, "Did you hear that? Did you hear that? She jumped up and clapped her hands. That will happen to me. I'm going to be baptized soon, and I'll be able to hear just like that old lady."

Mom and Dad looked at each other and said, "Well, um, you never know. Maybe so. Whatever God's plan is for you."

"I know I will be able to hear," Aimee replied.

For the next few months before Aimee's baptism, Cam and Patsy kept hearing Aimee talking about the possibility of being able to hear. Finally, Aimee turned eight years old, and the day of her baptism arrived. Bishop Doty conducted the baptism, which was held at the North Hollywood stake center, a church building on Saticoy Street. The curtains to the baptistery were locked, and the church leaders had to scramble to find keys to open it. The person with the assignment to fill the font forgot to take care of it, and the only way to get the font filled in time was to use all cold water. A huge crowd of family, relatives, and close friends filled the primary room until there was standing room only.

Wearing a beautiful white dress, Aimee walked out of the bathroom and into the font. Aimee said to her mom, "I can't wait to hear. I know that as soon as I'm baptized, I'll be able to hear."

Patsy reassured Aimee, "Whatever happens will be fine. You will be fine. Life will be wonderful."

As Aimee walked down the font steps, she noticed that the water was cold, just like lake water. She hugged her dad and looked out over all of the friends and family who attended her baptism. She noticed Granddad Clinger and Grandpa Walker who served as witnesses, her cousin Angela who had played the prelude music, Heather who would play a special musical number, and cousin Rahny who would play the postlude music. Even her teacher, Elizabeth Alda, who was not a member of the Church, sat in the audience, serving as an interpreter for the service.

Cam felt concern about the pressure that had been created for Aimee to be healed during her baptism because of the mission president's story, but he knew that Aimee had the faith for it to happen if it were Heavenly Father's will. Cam baptized Aimee, and as she came out of the water, everything was still. Aimee hugged her father, and she looked around at all of her family and friends—with a big smile on her face—waiting. She slowly realized that she couldn't hear, and Cam signed to her, "I'm so proud of you."

As the witnesses began to close the curtain to the baptismal font, Aimee signed back, "I'm so happy. I feel the Spirit. I feel warm. It's okay. It's all right." Cam didn't understand what "It's okay" meant until he reached the top of the stairs leading out of the font: Aimee is deaf, and that's okay. That's all right. Heavenly Father has a plan for her. Aimee has a mission.

Later, Aimee explained to her parents the impression that the Spirit gave her after her baptism: "Don't worry. You'll be fine. You'll have a great life. You will be able to help others, so be happy with who you are. It's okay to be deaf. You won't be able to hear, but in heaven you will hear." This revelation was clear, strong, and positive.

After receiving this message, Aimee knew that she was not going to be able to hear, and she felt grateful to be who she was. She felt love for herself, happiness, and gratitude for the way God made her. She appreciated her life and she thought, Maybe I can help other people.

Aimee's father blessed her with the gift of the Holy Ghost that same day. Most of the men in the room stood in the circle to bless Aimee, and each priesthood holder could hardly get a finger on Aimee's head. After bestowing the gift of the Holy Ghost, Cam talked about Aimee's mission. The Spirit helped Aimee to understand the promise she was making and the gift she was receiving. She realized that the guidance of the Spirit would help her and assist her to helping others make good decisions. The same warm assurance again enveloped her—only stronger now—and revealed that she was going to be okay no matter what happened. She understood that her wonderful family would be able to support her in anything that she had to do.

In the car on the way home from the baptism, Patsy asked Aimee, "How do you feel about being baptized and receiving the gift of the Holy Ghost?"

"It's the greatest birthday gift I could ever have," said Aimee. Patsy started crying.

"Do you want to know why it's the greatest birthday gift?" Aimee said. "Because finally now I understand. God has a plan for me. I can live and be happy. Nothing can stop me. I can become successful with whatever I do, and I can help other people too."

Aimee's baptism was one of the greatest days of her life, and after it, she stopped saying, "I wish I could hear." Of course, she has missed certain things. She would like to hear music and the voices of her family and friends, but she looks forward to that day when she can hear people's voices, amazing music, and angels singing in heaven. But after Aimee's baptism, her focus shifted to her mission, and she thought about herself in that light from then on.

7 **First Kiss**

In 1991, Aimee was in the Tripod program, which included a combination of deaf and hearing children at Washington Elementary School in Burbank, California. In October, the producers of *Baywatch,* a popular television show, came to Tripod looking for a deaf girl or boy about the age of eight to be a guest star in an episode called "Big Monday." Greg Bonann directed the show. Calling on his experience as a former lifeguard, Greg knew first hand about the inconsolable nature of mothers of children who have disappeared at the beach, and he knew that not being able to hear would add drama to the story of a drowning victim. The script for the episode told the story of an ocean rescue of a deaf child born to hearing parents, and the parents were opposed to their child learning American Sign Language because they wanted the child to learn to speak and be part of the oral world. Unable to speak or sign, the child had no way to communicate.

Many boys and girls came to the audition to try out, but the producers quickly learned that the role was too big for a deaf child actor with no acting experience. As a result, they signed a contract with a hearing child with acting experience to play the role of the deaf child in the episode. When members of the Deaf community caught wind of this, they became outraged. They felt it was like hiring a white actor to play the role of a black person: insulting. Under pressure from the Deaf community, the producers asked the Deaf community if they would be satisfied if they gave a deaf child a screen test as a trial to see if he or she could handle the significant role in the episode, and the Deaf community agreed.

Out of all the kids at the initial audition, the producers liked Aimee the best, so they invited her to the screen test. They threw her into the hardest part of the role, anticipating that she would fail, and the opportunity would appease the Deaf community. After all, they had signed a contract with a hearing girl to play the role of the deaf child.

In "Big Monday," after being rescued from the ocean, the deaf child is sitting on a couch in the lifeguard office. Her mother is on the phone making arrangements for the father to pick them up. A hearing woman played by Pamela Bach, who knows American Sign Language and who witnessed the rescue, starts communicating with the girl, "Your name is Lili," and she finger spells "L-I-L-I," looking at the bewildered child. The mother hangs up the phone, approaches the couch, slides Lili away from the woman, and sits down between them, explaining that Lili doesn't understand American Sign Language. The woman says, "If you'd like her to learn, I have some friends that run a school, and they can teach your whole family to sign."

"No—thank you," the mother replies. "We don't believe in that. We want Lili to grow up normal, not have other people treat her as though she is different."

The woman says, "Mrs. Seeger, Lili *is* different, and that's not bad. But she is deaf, and she needs a way to express to you what she thinks and how she feels and the things that she wants. Learning sign language can open up a whole new world for her."

As the mother justifies her objection to Lili learning American Sign Language, a large fish tank catches Lili's attention, and she walks over and admires the colorful fish. Lili walks back to her mom, grabs her mom's shoulders, and starts shaking them, babbling some incoherent noises, then pointing at the fish tank. The mother says, "What is it? What is it?" Lili's noises and shaking escalate at the mother's incomprehension—to the point that the mother has to restrain her daughter to stop the tantrum, which creates an embarrassing moment.

The woman interrupts, "Please, Mrs. Seeger, I think I know what she wants. Can I take her?" The mother reluctantly acquiesces.

At the aquarium, the woman uses simple signs to decipher Lili's desire: to feed the fish. As Lili drops fish food into the tank, she smiles. The woman turns to the mother and points out, "You know, Mrs. Seeger, if she knew sign language, she would have been able to tell us exactly what she wanted to do." The mother looks at Lili without responding.

Cam took Aimee to the screen test, and the screen test went so well that the producers selected Aimee for the part, which meant giving the hearing girl a role as an extra, but having to pay her as if she had kept the key role of the deaf girl.

Since Aimee had learned American Sign Language late, Cam filled the director in on how angry and frustrated Aimee would become before she learned to express herself through signs. The writers of the show lacked the personal experience to make the scene accurate, so they made adjustments in the script based on what Cam told them.

On the day of the actual filming, a cast and crew of about forty to fifty people gathered on Will Rogers State Beach on a cold, clear day in late October, and Patsy supported Aimee in her part. The crew filmed Aimee wandering into the water and pretending to drown. Underwater cameras shot the scene. The deaf tech wouldn't go into the cold water, so Patsy, wearing a wetsuit, entered the water up to her shoulders. Aimee couldn't wear a wetsuit for the filming, so she was shivering. David Hasselhoff, playing the role of a lifeguard, then raced into the ocean to rescue her. After he carried her limp body to shore and placed her on the sand, he bent down to give her mouth-to-mouth resuscitation. As he was about to cover Aimee's mouth, she jumped up, walked several feet away, and signed, "No, no, no, I'm not going to do that. I refuse. It's not the right time. I have to wait until I'm married. Nobody is going to touch my lips until I'm married. I'm not going to have sex with anyone." Of course, only Patsy understood Aimee's frantic signs.

Patsy thought, Oh, my gosh. Here they took a chance on a little deaf child, and they are going to wish they had stuck with the hearing girl.

Patsy then signed to Aimee, "Please, Aimee. Please, Aimee. This is acting. Just go lie back down. It's okay. He is not kissing you. Don't worry. We'll go shopping at the mall!" Patsy looked at the cast and crew, and thought, What are we doing here? Finally, Aimee agreed.

David carried her back to the spot with the cameras rolling. He put his mouth down on her again, and she bolted away again, signing, "No, no, no." Some of the crew members were dying with laughter.

Patsy signed, "Please. Please. All these people. You have no idea what a problem this is. I know you can do this."

Greg Bonann, the director, walked over to Patsy and said, "Are we going to be able to get this shot?"

Patsy replied, "Oh, yeah. No problem. It's really my mistake: in preparing for this shot, I explained to her that he really wouldn't touch her mouth."

He said, "I have a lot of people here, and we need to move on."

"I know. I know," Patsy said.

The third time was a charm, and Aimee held still for David's mouth-to-mouth resuscitation. After the third time, Greg said, "She's got it. That's perfect."

Aimee signed, "That's it. I'll never, never . . . kiss anybody again—only my husband."

Patsy thought, Hey, what's the big deal? I'll trade places with you. But then she realized that Cam wouldn't appreciate that.

When Aimee's friends ask her about her first kiss, she has to say, "David Hasselhoff."

They say, "Isn't he a little old for you?" And she has to explain.

The "Big Monday" episode of *Baywatch* led to two other invitations to come back and act in the series, and it paved the way for Aimee to act in other videos: *How to Talk to a Deaf Person* and *Little Girls in Pretty Boxes.* Although Aimee was invited to act in other movies, *Baywatch* was the first and most significant because it provided a forum to inspire a large audience: ABC News reported that "At the peak of its popularity, '*Baywatch*' was the most-watched television series in the world, with more than 1.1 billion viewers tuning in each week to see the Los Angeles lifeguards jog in slow motion."

A positive consequence of getting to be on *Baywatch* was the relationship that developed between the costume designer, Karen Braverman-Freeman, and the Walkers. Karen grew up in Long Island, and her Jewish ancestors immigrated to the United States from Russia. Karen rose quickly in the field of costume design, working shows like *Charles in Charge, Nightrider,* and *Baywatch.* When Karen met Aimee, who was deaf, who was blind in one eye, and who belonged to The Church of Jesus Christ of Latter-day Saints, she immediately felt attracted to her and the Walkers. With time their friendship grew, and Karen donated *Baywatch* shirts that she paid for herself to an auction fundraiser at the Tripod school that Aimee attended. Karen joined the Walkers at their home and church for various events and noticed the tolerance and respect that the Walkers had for people of other faiths and the optimism with which they embrace life.

When Karen's husband, Dr. L. Wayne Freeman, an ophthalmologist specializing in cataracts and glaucoma, learned about Aimee performing gymnastics at a high level while being deaf and blind in one eye, he wanted to see her perform. After one performance, he said, "It's not possible for her to do what she does—because of the loss of depth perception with only one eye and the loss of balance through deafness. On paper, it's not possible."

Aimee and her brother Jamie shared a room, and they slept on a trundle bed. Aimee slept on the lower bed, and Jamie slept on the upper bed. When it was time to go to sleep, Cam or Patsy would enter the room and say, "Lights Out. It's bedtime." Jamie and Aimee would still want to talk, so they started a tradition. They turned the lights out, said goodnight to their parents, and then signed into each other's hands in the dark, tactile sign language, the way that Helen Keller did it. Jamie would sign into Aimee's hands, and then Aimee would sign into Jamie's hands. If Aimee didn't understand Jamie's signs, she would grab his hands and hold them—meaning it's not clear: start over. If Jamie wanted to start over, he would wave his hand back and forth as if he was erasing a board. They even created their own dialect of American Sign Language, and they grew very close in the process.

During the day, Jamie served as Aimee's eyes and ears. For example, after school one day in junior high when Aimee was waiting to be picked up, a group of boys stood behind her, making fun of the way that she sounded and the noises she made when she tried to use her voice. Then they started acting as if they had disabilities, disfiguring their hands at their chests and making facial expressions to match. They howled with laughter as they mocked Aimee behind her back—until Jamie charged the leader, blindsiding him, knocking him off his feet, and dropping him to the ground. With a red face, Jamie screamed, "That's my sister! She can't help it!" After Jamie shoved a second boy, the group dispersed.

As the Walker kids grew up, one of their favorite movies was the 1960 Disney film *Swiss Family Robinson*, in which a shipwrecked family must survive on a deserted island, and they do so by building an elaborate treehouse. The Walkers always looked forward to visiting the Swiss Family Treehouse, a walk-through attraction at Disneyland, in Anaheim, California. One summer, the kids decided to build a treehouse in the Chinese elm tree in front of the house, and Danny, who was eighteen, led the way. They improvised with tools and supplies, using scrap wood, 2x4s, plywood, a twin mattress, and a futon bed. As the neighbors noticed the project developing, they started donating supplies. The first level looked like a huge box with lattice walls, and Jamie came up with the idea of converting part of the floor into a drawbridge that could be retracted to prevent neighborhood kids from entering the treehouse and falling out of it when it was unattended. The second level provided a sleeping area in one direction, and the third level provided another sleeping area in a different direction surrounded by Plexiglass. The boys sprayed Raid all over the treehouse so spiders wouldn't bite them as they slept at night. One evening, the family ran an orange extension cord into the tree house to power a lamp, a black-and-white TV, and a popcorn maker, and they watched *I Love Lucy*—and laughed and laughed—before falling asleep. Cam, Patsy, and Aimee slept on the top level while Danny slept on the middle level. Jamie and Brody slept on the bottom level; Brody was their fifty-pound springer spaniel and chocolate-lab mixed dog that had to be carried up the rope ladder and through the drawbridge. Those on the top level suffered from a giant street light shining in their eyes all night. Cam didn't sleep a wink that night, but he recollects saying, "Some people take their families to the Ritz Carlton; we take ours to the treehouse"—a monument to family fun.

On January 17, 1994, Aimee was 10, and even though she had been sharing a room with her brother Jamie, he was away spending the night at his cousin's house in Palmdale. News about "The Night Stalker," a serial killer named Richard Ramirez who was terrorizing southern Californians, had spooked Danny, and he didn't want to sleep alone. So he thought he would be a good big brother and offer to sleep in Jamie's bed to be near Aimee so she wouldn't get scared at night. Aimee loved the idea, and they eventually went to sleep on the trundle bed, with Aimee on the lower level and Danny on the upper level. At 4:30 a.m., Brody, the family dog—started barking. Then the house started shaking and creaking. Aimee slept soundly—partly because she heard nothing and partly because her gymnastics workouts that day had exhausted her.

Danny immediately woke up, grabbed Aimee, pulled her out of her lower bed and into his upper bed, and shielded her with his body as the large TV and dresser fell forward, crashing onto the lower bed from which Aimee had just been snatched.

"It's the Second Coming!" yelled Patsy.

Actually, it was the Northridge earthquake of '94—a 6.7 magnitude quake that rocked southern California, damaging 40,000 buildings, leaving 20,000 people homeless, injuring 8,700, and killing 57—a lot of damage for a quake that lasted only 15 seconds. Property damage was estimated at more than $20 billion. The earthquake rattled the Walker home too. Books, cups, plates, and pictures fell from shelves, counters, and cabinets and scattered shards of glass everywhere. The brick fence in the backyard collapsed, but all the members of the family were accounted for, and Danny's quick reaction had saved Aimee from being crushed or killed.

8 *Little Girls in Pretty Boxes*

Fritz Reiter ran Gymnastica Olympica where Aimee progressed rapidly through levels 6, 7, and 8. By this period, Aimee attended school from 8:00 a.m. to 3:00 p.m. and practice from 4:00 p.m. to 8:00 p.m. In the summer, the athletes practiced six to seven hours each day.

On one occasion, the girls stole Aimee's favorite Sunrise Surprise backpack that she had received as a birthday gift from her parents when she turned eleven. When it wasn't in her locker where she had put it, she started crying. She told coach Fritz, and he called the girls together. In his Austrian accent, he said, "Who took Aimee's backpack?" No one responded.

This wasn't the first time Aimee had been bullied. She liked to take power-naps at the gym when she had a break during long summer practices, and one day when she was asleep, a couple of the girls threw spaghetti on her face. Waking up immediately, Aimee realized what the girls had done to her as they stood at a distance, laughing. She felt sad and alone. When she told Fritz, he said, "I don't want any trouble." He knew what was happening, but he couldn't control it.

Some of the girls picked on anyone who was different, and Aimee was different. Because she couldn't hear, Fritz had to spend a little more time with her than the other girls. When hearing girls were on the bars, he could yell, "Keep your head down and your legs straight." When he had to correct Aimee, he would need to wait until after the routine and then communicate in broken American Sign Language. He also had a doll that he used in practice to help him show body postures in different positions, and he used the doll with everyone—but more so with Aimee.

Often, the girls would invite each other over for sleepovers. They would hide their sleeping bags at the gym because Aimee was never invited.

Aimee's natural talent and meteoric rise through the levels only made the situation worse.

However, Aimee was not the only one who was different and got picked on. A talented orthodox Jewish girl, Hannah, joined the gym, and the girls were so mean to her that she finally left the gym and never came back. But with Hannah gone, Aimee was the current target.

One of the incidences occurred when Aimee was injured. She had broken the metatarsal bone in her left foot, and she was wearing a bright pink boot to practice. Aimee still had to practice giant swings on the bars, and she had been chalking up. Someone said, "Go," so Aimee jumped up to the bar and was hanging. One of the other girls felt that it was her turn and walked up to Aimee on her right side, which is her blind side, and pulled her off the bar, causing her to land on her injured foot, re-injuring it and causing her to cry in pain.

One day, some of the older girls who were friends with Aimee came up to Patsy crying and saying, "Please take your daughter out of here. The other girls are so mean."

Finally, when Aimee was at level 9, all the parents called a meeting in the boardroom and invited Patsy to attend. About a dozen people sat around an oval table; no girls were there. The purpose of the meeting soon became apparent to Patsy.

The other parents went around the room saying things like, "My daughter has only been able to practice her floor routine twice while Aimee has been able to practice her floor routine four times" and "Communication with Aimee takes too much time from coaches—time that could be spent on other girls." A few times, Patsy spoke up to respond, and Fritz hushed her: he wanted all the other parents to have a turn first. Each parent took a turn expressing the injustice his or her daughter had endured at the hands of Aimee. They felt that one of the coaches, Jennifer, had played into Aimee's needs and lacked elite coaching skills; therefore, she should be replaced with a coach that could get their daughters to the Olympics.

Patsy held back her tears. Fritz looked around the room and then spoke up: "I'm really shocked at all of you. You are using Aimee as a way to get rid of Jennifer, and Jennifer is capable under my direction of coaching all of your girls. As far as Aimee goes, she is a bright light in this gym. She is wonderful to everyone. She is a great gymnast. I talk your girls through everything that they do. When they are on the bars, I give them constructive criticism. That's 100 times more beneficial than what I have to do with Aimee—communicating with her after the event. Your girls benefit so much more than Aimee from what we do here at the gym. Aimee is learning a new routine and can't hear the music. She needs a little extra time. You are wrong, we are a team, and I'm disappointed in all of you."

Patsy recognized that recent "beat-the-odds" newspaper stories and features on television news about Aimee had fueled the fire of jealousy. So among other things, she said, "Would any one of you want to change places with me? Would you want your daughter to be deaf? Is that what you would want to get this recognition?" No one responded.

Patsy lost it in the car on the drive home and started crying, providing only a simple explanation to Aimee about what happened: "We need to use the coaches less so that they have more time for the other girls."

The very next day, one of the mothers from the board meeting called Patsy to apologize: "I'm so sorry. Can you forgive us? We are very competitive and selfish and only think about how it benefits us. You and Aimee are different; you're not like that. So, it may be hard for you to understand us. Please, please forgive us. I'm sorry that I was at the meeting." Other apologies in various forms followed by other parents who attended the meeting.

In October 1996, Aimee was thirteen. Kathy Johnson, captain of the U.S. gymnastics team in the 1984 Olympics in Los Angeles, was working as the gymnastics technical advisor for Lifetime's television film *Little Girls in Pretty Boxes* based on the book of the same name by Joan Ryan, which is an indictment of the parents and coaches creating elite athletes in gymnastics and figure skating through damaging practices. The producers of the movie and Kathy Johnson approached several gyms, including Gymnastica Olympica, looking for actors. The script had four roles for gymnasts, and one of them was a role for a deaf gymnast. Aimee already had a screen actor's card from appearances on *Baywatch* and commercials, and she was the only deaf gymnast performing at a high level.

The audition first involved Aimee performing gymnastics skills to see if she performed at a high enough level to play the role of a champion gymnast. After the performance test, the producers interviewed Aimee. First, they said, "Do you love gymnastics?"

"Oh, yes," Aimee signed.

Then, they asked, "Do you like acting?"

Again Aimee signed, "Oh, yes."

They said, "Well, what are you, a gymnast or an actress?"

Aimee replied, "I'm a deaf gymnast and a deaf actress, and I'm proud of both." Then she added, "And I can sing too." Patsy thought, What are you doing, Aimee?

They said, "Oh, we have to hear this."

So, Aimee sang "Row, Row, Row, Your Boat." When she got to the word "boat," she pointed to her butt. The producers laughed and laughed.

Afterward, Patsy said, "You've got to lose the 'butt' part. I don't like that."

The producers were impressed with Aimee's personality, so they gave her the part. One week later, they called a read-through meeting with the actors to review the entire script, which took a couple of hours. They sat around an oval table, and Aimee had the script in her hands. All of her parts were highlighted in yellow. In the script, they had the character that Aimee played, Dianna, way off track during her floor routine because she couldn't hear the music. Aimee objected vehemently in the meeting: "No. No. No. That never happens to me. If you want to have me fall off the beam, that's fine, but I'm never off track with the music."

Kathy Johnson chimed in. "She's right. Why would the father give up his career to support his daughter if she can't even follow the music?" So the producers changed the script.

Aimee had to talk with Coach Fritz because she would be missing some practices, and he knew that the movie shed a critical light on figure skating and gymnastics. Initially, Fritz said, "No." Although Fritz didn't like the idea of Aimee missing practice, he learned that the movie gave several of the other girls in the gym opportunities to play minor roles as gymnasts. Since they couldn't be paid for gymnastics, the money, about $5,500, had to be donated to Gymnastica Olympica. Also, the girls would wear the Gymnastica Olympica (G.O.) leotards in the movie, and Jennifer, who was the real target at "the conspiracy meeting," would be hired to be a coach in the movie. When Kathy Johnson urged Fritz to support the movie, he reluctantly did.

Once the filming started, Aimee missed practice almost every day for one month. The producers provided a teacher on the set because she missed so much of the beginning of sixth grade at John Muir Middle School. Aimee could only be paid for the days that she acted, not performed gymnastics, to remain eligible for a college scholarship. Kathy Johnson proved invaluable to the girls in her role as liaison between the various interests. For example, the producers weren't aware of the dangers of distractions like lights and flashing cameras when girls were performing difficult tricks.

The filming took place in a YMCA gym. The producers had transformed the basketball court at the YMCA into a high-quality gymnastics gym—including a parent's room and a coach's office. Jamie Dantzscher was one of the athletes in the film whose path would later cross with Aimee's. Vanessa Atler was the stunt double for the main character. Aimee was thirteen, and she looked up to Jamie and Vanessa who were very successful and a little older, so working with them was a thrill. Aimee was a new level 10, and they were both elite. Both of them attended Charter Oak Gymnastics and were coached by Steve Rybacki. Both Steve Rybacki and Hal Halverson from Verdugo Gymnastics spotted Aimee since Fritz never came. Hal noticed that Aimee had long grasshopper legs, flexibility, and grace. During "school time," both of them learned a little American Sign Language.

One of the tricks Aimee had to perform on film was a flick layout on the beam, and she had to fall off the beam. After focusing on doing it perfectly at G.O., it took some planning to fail. The trick was not hurting herself in the fall. After her fall, she had to apologize to the coach, which gave him the opportunity to reply, "There are no apologies in the Olympics!" The lights were an even bigger challenge. Aimee's right eye can't see any objects, but it is sensitive to light. Bright light shown into her blind eye makes it hard for her to see in her good eye, which kept happening during the filming. A couple of times, the shot wouldn't work, and the camera crew had to shift to Aimee's left side to capture the scene. Also, flashes kept coming from the spectators to represent photos being taken, which of course is not allowed in real competitions, but those flashes created a problem for Aimee as well.

There were communication problems too. Jennifer had picked up some incorrect signs working at G.O. with Aimee, and Aimee just learned to understand Jennifer's own signs. However, during the filming, Patsy noticed Jennifer signing incorrectly, so she stopped the filming and said to the director, "Jennifer is using incorrect signs, and everyone will see that in the movie. Can I take a minute to show her the right signs?"

Patsy pulled Jennifer into a side room to explain a phrase in the script: "piece of cake," which Jennifer had been trying to sign literally. If, for example, Jennifer signs, "a flick layout is a piece of cake," she is saying "a flick layout is a serving of dessert." People will think she is crazy. Idioms don't always translate from one language to another. She has to sign, "A flick layout is easy." Jennifer eventually took to the acting, and halfway through the movie, she quit G.O.

From time to time, Patsy would step away from Aimee and when she returned, Aimee would be teaching a gymnastic skill or explaining a simple sign like "golf" or "jaws" in an entertaining way. The crew would be laughing hysterically. During make-up, members of the crew would come up to Aimee and write her little notes. Aimee's effervescent personality emerged, and she made social connections with the cast and crew.

At one point, the producer approached Patsy and said, "I would love to stay in contact with you and watch Aimee's career because at some point we would like to make a movie about Aimee herself."

Steve Rybacki came up to Patsy and asked her if Aimee was performing at an elite level. Patsy said, "No, she just started level 10."

Steve said, "She has the potential to be an elite gymnast, but she has to be in the right gym. You should come to Charter Oak." In the movie, this is exactly what Greg Ratkin, the head coach, said to recruit the main character, and he pushed his athletes too hard—to the point where they took painkillers and the main character broke her neck pushing herself in the gym. Seeing a line between fiction and reality can be difficult.

After the movie came out in the spring of 1996, Fritz wouldn't watch it, even though there were advertisements for it all over the place—on billboards and television. The Lifetime channel played it over and over because the Olympics in Atlanta were

LITTLE GIRLS IN PRETTY BOXES

approaching, and gymnastics is one of the most-watched events in the summer Olympics. One day at G.O., Fritz came up to Aimee who was not doing something well enough and yelled in his Austrian accent, "What would Greg Ratkin say?" When Patsy heard this, she burst into a fit of unstoppable laughter. Fritz was alluding to the antagonist in *Little Girls in Pretty Boxes*, which could only mean one thing—he had seen the movie.

Aimee's part in *Little Girls in Pretty Boxes* led to a positive relationship with Hal Halverson, and Aimee eventually left Fritz and G.O. and joined Hal's gym, Golden State Verdugo Gymnastics. Hal took skills that Aimee had and incorporated them into unique combinations to raise her points in competitions. Hal pushed his athletes, but not to the point of abuse. He had a good sense of humor. For example, Aimee was famous for over-chalking her hands. At one competition, she used so much chalk that a thin layer covered the floor beneath the bars. When Aimee fell off the bars, she left a print of her behind on the mat because of all the chalk dust. When Hal saw Aimee's derrière print, he started laughing and laughing—right in the middle of a meet. Hal made practices fun, too, through games like gymnastics H-O-R-S-E in which each girl would compete on one skill like sticking a landing off the bars. The girls would take turns, and each girl who missed the landing got a letter, "H" then "O" then "R," etc. When they got to "E," they had to stand on the side of the bars and cheer on those who were left, which created unity on the team. Hal made gymnastics fun, and he focused on building team cohesion. Sometimes practices went long because he and the girls would get lost in the games and lose track of time. Hal solicited the best from each athlete because the atmosphere was so positive and fun, which was unlike anything Aimee had experienced in other gyms.

In February 1998, Hal took his team to the Hawaiian ATT International Invitational. Grandma Clinger donated $840 to make the trip possible for Aimee and Patsy. After training the first night in Honolulu, Hal took the team out to eat at the Hard Rock Café; he didn't establish any diet restrictions. The café was very crowded, and rock star albums, clothes, and memorabilia covered the walls. Aimee noticed a large picture of Elvis Presley on the wall. Classic rock blared from the speakers, and Aimee could feel the base vibrations in her plate and see vibration rings in her drink.

During dinner, Hal said, "Come on Krystle, do a handstand on the table!"

Krystle sighed—as if to say, "Not this again." Krystle Wong was 4' 8" with beautiful skin, dimples, and long eyelashes.

"Come on, I want to see a handstand," repeated Hal.

The team knew the routine because Hal had made the request so many times. Krystle had performed a handstand at a teammate's birthday party on the edge of a stone bridge eighteen feet above a miniature golfing hole at Bullwinkle's. Krystle had performed a handstand after a meet on the edge of a bridge twenty-five feet above the water at Beinheim Palace in England, where Winston Churchill was born, which seemed to mock the gargoyles in frozen vigil on the palace walls. Hal had even requested a handstand from Krystle as he shamelessly promoted his gymnastics business at the Burbank Chamber of Commerce, knowing full well that while city officials would quickly forget his words, they would never forget Krystle in her leotard doing a handstand on top of the presenter's table.

Why not the Hard Rock Café in Hawaii too?

The team cleared everything away. Krystle climbed up on the table, bent over, pressed her hands onto the table, and slowly raised her legs into the air. She held her legs straight up and still.

Most gymnasts keep their balance in a handstand by moving their hands around on the mat; Krystle grips the mat with her fingers and finds the center of gravity in the middle of her palms. Then, she holds still like a statue; her record is three minutes. She's never lost a handstand contest in her life.

People from other tables at the Hard Rock Café gathered around and started clapping. As the seconds passed, everyone cheered. When Krystle came down, her face was red, but she could have held it all night—without flinching.

In the Hawaiian competition, Aimee made it to the finals and took third place on floor and fourth place on the bars in open optionals (level 10 and elite). After the competition, the gymnasts had a luau on the beach in which all the athletes from around the world talked, exchanged small gifts, and started pen pal relationships.

On the last day, Hal took his team surfing. The girls noticed that the surfing instructor was tall and well built, with dark skin, dark hair, and dark eyes—a native Hawaiian with an aloha smile. He worked out of a shack, and he would place a surfboard on a bench two feet above the sand. Then he would have the girls lie on the surfboard and practice popping up into a standing position. He laughed a lot as he taught the girls. He showed them how to ride waves on a longboard, and they all did well because gymnasts are short and athletic with a good sense of balance. Aimee wore a one-piece blue-green bathing suit and an orange rashguard that covered her arms and upper body. Her blond hair hung in a ponytail. She rode a blue ten-foot surfboard with a leash. The water looked crystal clear and felt warm, and she could see colorful fish beneath the surface. A net in the water kept the sharks out of the surfing area, so Aimee and her teammates would be fine as long as they didn't slice their feet on the coral bottom. The surfing instructor—the big kahuna—took Aimee and Patsy so far out into the water that Aimee could no longer see the shore. She wondered what she had gotten herself into. Still, Aimee overcame her fears, applied what she knew from gymnastics, and caught several waves—riding them nearly to the shore—but her mother outdid her by riding a wave on a yellow board all the way to the sand. The Beach Boys in "Catch a Wave," a hit from their 1963 album *Surfer Girl*, best described the thrill that Patsy and Aimee felt that day: "Catch a wave and you're sittin' on top of the world."

9 Russia

After Aimee and her teammates returned from Hawaii, they competed at the Golden State Invitation meet in Burbank. After Aimee's floor routine, Coach Hal said, "Come here. I have someone very important I want you to meet." International elite judge and coach, Olga Mataganova, approached Aimee and Patsy with tears in her eyes and said, "I appreciated watching you. You are so wonderful, and you are deaf. You finish your routines on time with the music. You are an inspiration to me." Olga was from Almaty, Kazakhstan, a former Soviet Republic in Central Asia. The Russians were in the practice of screening out people with disabilities, placing them in institutions, and denying them opportunities. Olga continued, "You have a wonderful mother who supports you and allows you to train. With parents like that, you have opportunities, and you are lucky."

Olga continued, "We are having the first Nellie Kim Cup, an international invitational in Kazakstan with gymnasts from around the world, and we want you to come. All the gymnasts are elite, and we know you are not, but we don't care. We want you to be there." The invitation came directly from Nellie

Kim, five-time Olympic gold medalist who would become elected president of the Women's Artistic Gymnastics Technical Committee in 2004, making her the top technical person in women's gymnastics in the world.

Olga was so impressed with Aimee that she wrote out Aimee's entire routine in her judging language, which is like hieroglyphics, and she told Aimee exactly what her routine was worth and how she could earn bonuses by leaping higher and including connections in her routine. Olga calculated that with minor improvements, Aimee would be able to compete with other elite gymnasts without having an embarrassing experience. Hal, Patsy, and Aimee told Olga that they wanted to go if it were possible.

Lonnie Levitt worked for CBS news and wanted to share Aimee's story. She prepared a seven-minute video for television. At the end of the video, a voiceover explained how to donate money in order to send Aimee and her coach to Russia to represent the U.S.A. One of the owners of Lucky Jeans saw the news segment on television and contacted Coach Hal, asking him to draw up a budget and submit it to him. Later, the owner contacted Hal to explain that Lucky Jeans would be donating enough money to cover 100% of the budget that he had created for the trip to Russia. That was a $6,000 donation, but about another $1,000 came in through other contributions. One woman sent in a letter that said, "I just barely bought a Princess Diana Beanie Baby." It was a purple bear, a collector's item, and she continued, "I'm donating it to be sold to help pay for Aimee's trip." It brought in $300. Grandma Walker insisted on making a donation of $200 from her social security income. Sallie Weaver from Gym-Kin donated all the leotards and warm-ups.

One boy sent in a letter with $4.25 (four one-dollar bills and a quarter taped to the letter). In pencil in child-print, he had written, "Aimee, here is a little bit of money for Russia. You can do it. Go for the Gold." Coach Hal and the Walkers were so thankful for all the donations.

Cam gave Patsy and Aimee a blessing of safety before they

left, which helped the butterflies in Aimee's stomach. They left for Russia on September 2, 1998, Grandma Walker's birthday, and they brought cans of chicken and tuna and other food because they were unsure about what would be available. The luggage weighed so much that they had to pay extra. They picked up Hal on the way to the airport, and Aimee asked Hal if he would cut his mustache so she could read his lips. Hal pulled his upper lip out and said, "Here, is that better?" He made up his own signs and loved to tease Aimee and be goofy.

They flew from LAX to Chicago where they transferred to a plane to Frankfurt. From there, they took another plane to Almaty, Kazakhstan. A 400-pound man sat between Hal and the Walkers on the last leg of their flight, and he was sweating most of the time, making the 26-hour trip covering 9,260 miles a challenge. It felt as if it took a week.

After exiting the plane, they noticed that everything looked small and old, nothing like LAX, and they noticed the military presence everywhere. The Walkers felt as though they were in a war zone, which made them uneasy. In the small airport, occasionally they would see a bare light bulb hanging from the ceiling. They could see a searchlight nearby. The airport workers and military didn't speak English, and they were trying to tell Coach Halverson and the Walkers where to go. The Walkers were frightened. Luckily, Olga and two men from the Russian Federation showed up. Olga said, "Don't say one word. We'll handle this. You are Americans. If you say the wrong thing, you could go to prison."

They got into a van without seatbelts and drove to their hotel. Drivers ran red lights. Pedestrians walked in the street. There appeared to be no rules on the road. People drove about 75 miles per hour in areas where 40 miles per hour seemed appropriate, and the roads themselves were small and in disrepair—unlike the freeway system in Los Angeles. The buildings were old, and the floors inside the hotel were uneven. They had to step over metal plates in the doorways. The hot water was not working: just freezing cold water. On each floor in the hallway of their hotel, two women sat in white dresses behind a table. Each time that Patsy and Aimee left their room, they had to forfeit their room key to one of these women, who stored it in a metal box on the table and retrieved it when they returned. Women in white stood guard twenty-four hours a day, rotating shifts. They looked skinny and strong with high cheekbones and pale skin. They documented all activity in a book: arrivals, departures, visitors, etc. The Walkers experienced many inconveniences: the television in the room may have been made in the 1950s. It took the Walkers five days before they could find access to a phone that worked, and they called Cam to let him know that their plane had landed safely. The Walkers wouldn't leave anything valuable in their room, and they wondered if the food was safe to eat. It was a different world.

Inside the room were two wooden beds, about twelve to fourteen inches off the ground, narrow and short, much smaller than twin beds, with tapestry coverings. The beds were as hard as rocks.

Patsy and Aimee left the room on their first day to exchange some of their American money for Russian money. After they had returned to their rooms, Patsy heard a fist pounding on the front door. With no peep-hole, she opened the door cautiously, and a lady pushed the door open, yelling, "Nyet. Nyet. Nyet." She was holding their American money, and she kept pointing to her calculator. Russian body language is strong, and Aimee is tuned into nonverbal cues. Aimee studied her gesticulating, angry face, and focused on the American dollars that the Walkers had exchanged for Kazakhstan tenges. Through Aimee's keen eye for reading expressions and her ability to improvise signs and pantomime, she managed to communicate with the two women. Patsy and Aimee had given American money that was brand new—crisp bills with a tint of color—which the Kazakhs apparently had never seen before because they thought it was counterfeit. Aimee signed to Patsy to exchange old bills for new bills, which Patsy did. The anger dissipated from the woman's face, they gave each other thumbs-up signs, and then they hugged each other. This exchange gave Aimee the opportunity to serve as interpreter and peacemaker.

As they were walking around the city, Aimee had to use the toilet, so they stopped in a restaurant. There was no door on the bathroom, and there was no toilet inside the bathroom, just a hole in the floor. Aimee had to stand, in a public place, and there was no toilet paper—just newspaper. Patsy stood guard in the doorway for Aimee. Fortunately, Patsy had some tissues with her, but this experience was awkward for Aimee.

All the people from the meet stayed in the same hotel, and they often ate breakfast together. The bread was soggy, and the poached eggs were a little strong and orange. The jello looked good: orange and clear, similar to tapioca pudding in consistency. Aimee put a spoonful of jello into her mouth, and Patsy just looked on in curiosity. It tasted disgusting, and she couldn't spit it out because the napkins were cloth. With a contorted face, Aimee signed, "What is that?"

Patsy just laughed and laughed. Aimee wanted to spit it out, but she didn't want to be rude. She looked for a trash can. Patsy finally said, "Do you know what that is? That's fish eggs."

"Are you serious? Why didn't you stop me from putting that in my mouth?"

Patsy signed through her laughter, "I just wanted to see how you would respond."

The caviar tasted salty and bitter—worse than a mouth full of sea water.

"How do people like that?" Aimee asked.

"It's very expensive," answered Patsy as she continued laughing.

"We're not buying it," Aimee said. "I'm going to get you back. Just wait."

"Okay, bring it on," Patsy replied. Each time throughout the day when Patsy thought of Aimee's caviar face, she burst into laughter.

After some sight-seeing, all the athletes and their coaches were brought to the training facility where the meet would take place. It was a five-story concrete building, and the gym was on the third floor. On the first day, Hal was the last person to enter the elevator, but there wasn't room for him. So he got out just in time; the elevator door grazed his face. The elevators there didn't retract when you put your hand out, and the elevator almost caught Hal's head. This scared Aimee, and she had a nightmare that an elevator door took off Hal's head. Blood was everywhere, and she woke up in a sweat and ran to the bathroom—to throw up. This dream reoccurred several times per month for two to three years and less often after that. To this day, Aimee doesn't like elevators. Even now, when Aimee enters an elevator—if she has to—she moves to the back and pulls others close to her.

The gymnastics equipment fueled Aimee's fears. The gym lacked soft mats; they felt as though they were filled with sawdust instead of foam. The lighting was poor, and the springboard for the vault lacked the usual spring that she knew in the United States. The bars were old, rigid, and too close, so they had to be adjusted. Hal and the Korean coach worked on adjusting the bars until they were sweating. The beam lacked spring and felt uneven, and the covering was worn out and slippery. For the first time in her life, Aimee used chalk on the beam.

Two days before the meet, Aimee was complaining about the equipment, and Hal pulled her aside and said, "Just be grateful that you have such great equipment in your gym at home. Just do your best here."

The day before the meet, they had a complete timed run-through of all the events with all the athletes, but it was not judged. On the vault, Aimee couldn't get her timing down on the runway. On the bars, Aimee missed her ginger—a release in which she flies away with a half-turn and then re-catches the bar—and she dropped from the high bar to the floor in a belly-flop position, which knocked the wind out of her. On her second attempt, she slipped off the bar in the middle of her undershoot over half-turn and fell onto the ground. On her third attempt, she fell again. The chalk was white, the walls were white, and the light was dim—all of which made it difficult for Aimee to see with one eye. Aimee started crying and freaked out—the only time that anxiety had overwhelmed her in her gymnastics career.

Hal took Aimee outside the gym, into the stairwell, grabbed her shoulders, leaned forward, and yelled, "You listen up." Patsy had followed and had to bend down and put on an angry face to interpret for Aimee. "You don't understand how lucky and blessed you are to be here. You are the first American to compete in Kazakhstan. You are here to inspire this crowd and these people, not act like a little two-year-old cry-baby. How old are you?"

"Fifteen," Aimee said.

"Fifteen. You are almost 16. Before you know it, you'll be 18. Stop acting like a baby." Then Hal started talking about a former athlete of his named Janine who was tough. "Janine faced challenges, and she never gave excuses. She didn't care how bad the equipment was. She was a champion. I want my champion here. I want you to go back out there and do it again. Show your best. Show these people who you are. You are Aimee Walker. I don't care if you fell. Pick yourself up. Don't show that you're afraid. Pretend like you're not afraid, like it didn't affect you. Stop crying. Dry those tears. Stop it right now. If you're going to cry, we're going home."

"No. No," Aimee signed. "I don't want to go home. I'm sorry. I'm sorry. I'm sorry."

"Stop saying you're sorry. I forgive you. It's over. Just go back and show me in there." Aimee wiped her eyes, grabbed her grips, and walked back into the gym.

Later, Hal pointed to Oksana Chusovitina, a Russian Olympian, and said to Aimee, "Go watch her on the bars. She is twenty-five. Her body is tired, but she keeps going. Her mind is amazing. She has teeth like a tiger." Oksana chalked up, without grips, and performed a great routine. Hal continued, "Your body is young. You're fifteen. She's twenty-five. You can do it. Be strong. Don't complain. She has many injuries, and she just got out of the hospital about ten days ago with appendicitis."

Throughout the day, Aimee thought about what Hal had said

and about Oksana. Then, Aimee started improving. Some of the other coaches noticed Aimee's progress and said, "Get over here. Give me a hug." Aimee started feeling better.

After Aimee finished a good floor routine, Hal told her to go back to the vault, which Aimee didn't want to do. Hal said, "No, you need to overcome your fear. Go on. You are a tiger."

Aimee went to the vault, said a prayer, and thought about Oksana. Aimee practiced several tricks, and her performance improved. Her mind started focusing on the positive: her confidence and courage started to return.

At the end of the day, Oksana walked over to Aimee. Aimee had watched Oksana on television in the Olympics and was in awe of her. Oksana, who was about the same height, put her arm around Aimee, pointed to Aimee, pointed to herself, and drew a heart on her chest—as if to say, "We love each other." Then, through improvised signs, she communicated, "Just be calm. Push it out of your mind. I'm watching you." A warm feeling enveloped Aimee.

As Patsy and Aimee were getting ready for bed later that night and reflecting on the day, Aimee said, "Thank you, Mom, for being there every minute and supporting me in gymnastics. I'm thankful for Hal. I'm happy now. I wasn't happy then, but he helped me realize that I had to stop crying. I had to show my skills. It opened my mind up. I'm sorry that it had to happen, but I'm glad that it did. I feel grateful for everything." She fell asleep and dreamed about gymnastics throughout the night: all the routines went well—no mistakes.

Several members of the press attended the practices and interviewed people and took photographs. After one of the practices, a member of the press interviewed Patsy. He asked, "Why would you think to give your daughter the opportunity to become a great gymnast when she has infirmities?"

Patsy was shocked at the question and answered, "She is my daughter, and of course I would give her any opportunity to enrich her life, and she loves gymnastics. I couldn't stop her." This message was carried to the people through newspapers and television.

On the first day of competition, as the first American gymnast to compete in Almaty, Kazakhstan, Aimee performed all of her routines well, but she displayed her prowess in her floor routine, her favorite event. She had an out-of-this-world feeling as she tumbled and danced across the mat. She felt extra power in her legs—like a deer—as she performed a round-off whip to a back handspring to a double-and-a-half twist, landing on her feet like a cat to the music of "Carmen." The crowd stood up and erupted in cheers as Aimee saluted the judges. As she rose from her bow, she saw that Nellie Kim had walked out onto the floor to give her a big hug. Aimee was in awe—an Olympic gold medalist and this was her meet, the inaugural of the Nellie Kim Cup. Aimee couldn't believe that this could happen to her.

There were many great moments in the meet involving elite and Olympic gymnasts—male and female athletes from around the world—when many people in the crowd rose to their feet in applause. However, there was only one moment in the entire meet when every single person in the building stood to cheer, and it was the only time that Nellie Kim walked out onto the floor to recognize an athlete during the meet, and that happened at the end of Aimee's floor routine. Nellie pointed to her own heart, then pointed to Aimee, and gave her a big hug. Nellie was in tears. Bruno Grandi—president of the Federation of International Gymnastics (FIG), the body that conducts the world championships and the Olympics—was in tears.

At the end of the day, all athletes who won first, second, or third place received awards and flowers. Aimee did not place in the top three in any event, but the top eight athletes in each event moved on to finals the next day, and Aimee qualified for finals in two events by placing sixth in floor and sixth in beam.

On the day of the finals, Aimee wore a burgundy crushed velvet leotard, and she competed on the beam first. The Russian crowd kept yelling, "Stoi!"—Stick it! Hal had a knack for creating a routine that played to Aimee's strengths, so he had modified her beam routine to include a front somersault mount onto the beam, back handspring to a layout back somersault and a punch front on the beam, and dismount with a gaining back somersault. Aimee's prior coaches had tried to teach her a roundoff double twist off the beam, but it terrified her, and Hal said to himself, "Why make a child with vision problems do a skill that requires vision?" So he changed her dismount from a back handspring into a double twist off the end of the beam to a side gainer into a double twist off the side of the beam—the same level of difficulty—but it played to her strengths. She stuck it.

The crowd went nuts, chanting, "Aimee, Aimee, Aimee." After Aimee waved to the crowd and walked away, Hal brought her back out and held her up by the waist above his head for the crowd—the way that Bela Karolyi did it.

During her floor routine, her tumbles went well, including her double pike double back, and she made a connection with the audience, revealing her personality in her dancing.

After the competition, the athletes exchanged pins and gifts and went to a special dinner concluding the first Nellie Kim Cup, including about thirty-five female and thirty-five male athletes from many nations with their coaches. White snowball flowers dressed each table.

After dinner when everyone quieted down, Bruno Grandi, FIG president, addressed everyone. In his Italian accent and broken English, he explained that he was so pleased with the first Nellie Kim Cup—a wonderful event—and he explained that it would continue. He said that they were honored that so many people could come from all over the world. He then started to explain that one person has made this whole event what it is and made all the difference, and he went on and on and on. Patsy thought, Oh, Nellie is amazing. And then Bruno said, "And this person is Aimee Walker from the U.S.A." Everyone cheered. Patsy was stunned and had mixed emotions. She felt chills of pride, but then thought, This is too much of a good thing. No, don't put all that focus on Aimee. Bruno continued, "Aimee has filled our hearts with the fire of warmth and love and inspired us all to become better."

After Bruno's talk, the athletes mingled and talked. Alexi, a Russian athlete from Kazakhstan, said to Aimee, "If you were older, I would date you." He was about twenty-two. Patsy smelled vodka, smiled, and thought, Over my dead body.

On the plane on the way home, Aimee started crying. She said to her mom, "I'm going to miss the people so much. I hope that they will open up those institutions and give those kids with disabilities a new life with opportunities now that they have seen me. What do you think? Do you think they will? I want to come back some day when I have the money and go inside the institutions and speak and encourage them to get out of there. I might be able to travel and tell them about challenges that I have overcome and help them."

Patsy started crying too and said, "I'll interpret for you. We'll go all over the world, and it will be great."

The airline stewardess noticed Patsy and Aimee crying and said, "Is everything okay?"

Patsy answered, "Yes, we're just so happy."

10 Citius. Altius. Fortius.

By 1999, Aimee and her family had made the decision to train with Coach Mary Wright in Utah, which meant splitting the family for long periods of time—with Dad in California and Mom and Aimee in Utah. The family carefully selected Mary Wright because of her credentials, and they believed that she could take Aimee to the Olympics. Mary ran Olympus School of Gymnastics in Sandy, Utah. Born in New Zealand, she spoke to her athletes with an accent, and she made short, positive comments. She had a God-given talent for seeing technical aspects of skills, giving apt feedback, and motivating girls. Short, polite, and passionate, she had already trained five of the eight girls on the 1984 Olympic team that had competed in Los Angeles. She often said, "Champions are made in practice" and "Fight to do it right." Her gym was equipped with video cameras with five-second delays, so the athletes could review their performances and see what she saw with the naked eye. Practices ran daily after school from 2:30 to 8:00 or 9:00 p.m., but the elite athletes also practiced before school from 6:00 to 7:00 a.m. three days a week. The gym had no heater, and Utah's snowy winter shivered Aimee's California frame. No athlete misunderstood the tone set by the Olympic motto inscribed on the gym wall: "Citius—Altius—Fortius." Faster. Higher. Stronger.

Aimee was a sophomore at Mountain View High School in Orem, Utah. Melanie Gurney also attended Mountain View, and she enrolled in an introductory American Sign Language class in 10th grade. Melanie noticed Aimee on campus, but only waved to her in the hallways because she felt self-conscious about her signing ability. After all, she couldn't even string together a sentence. In the introductory class, she had acquired a simple vocabulary, like the names of some foods and family members. In 11th grade, Melanie took the second American Sign Language class taught by Darlene King, who also interpreted for some of the deaf students on campus, including Aimee.

At the beginning of the year, Mrs. King pulled Melanie aside and said, "You need to get to know Aimee. Your personalities are so similar."

"No way, no way, no way," replied Melanie. That was too far outside of Melanie's comfort zone. Mrs. King didn't give up. Throughout the semester, she kept prompting Melanie to approach Aimee. Melanie kept declining.

Finally, after one project, Mrs. King said, "Your project looks great, and you have an 'A,' but if you want to keep the 'A,' you need to eat lunch with Aimee Walker."

Melanie mustered the courage to approach Aimee, who sat signing with four or five deaf students. Melanie felt as though her face was red because her vocabulary was so limited: she could only talk about her favorite foods and her family. Even the words that she did know, she couldn't remember because she was trying to eat, interpret, and sign—all while feeling very nervous. However, Aimee quickly put Melanie at ease with her patience. They talked about their families. Melanie explained that she had two brothers and three sisters, and she could explain one thing about each one, like "My oldest brother plays basketball." They tried to talk about their classes, but Melanie lacked the vocabulary. She had to resort to finger spelling. Aimee pulled out a notebook so Melanie could write words that she couldn't sign. Lunch flew by for both of them. Mrs. King was right: they had a lot in common.

They started eating lunch together almost every day, sometimes with Aimee's friends and sometimes with Melanie's friends. They also talked in the hallways, and this lasted the first half of their junior year. During the second half of that year, they became better and better friends. They started hanging out together on weekends and occasionally for short visits when Aimee returned from practice. Melanie learned American Sign Language rapidly through Aimee. By their senior year, they were inseparable.

From time to time, Melanie would go back to Mrs. King and ask how to communicate an idea in ASL, and Mrs. King watched the relationship grow with pleasure. Most of the other deaf and hearing students did not enter each other's worlds. They ate and socialized separately.

During Melanie and Aimee's senior year (2001-2002), they took a seminary class together where they studied the scriptures. Each year, Aimee's mother would interpret for Aimee in seminary, but during their senior year, Melanie interpreted for Aimee about half of the time, which forged a bond between them and catapulted Melanie's signing.

The seminary class started with prayer, and Aimee often volunteered. Melanie was in the habit of closing her eyes, folding her arms, and bowing her head during prayers, and often she fell into that habit while she was supposed to be interpreting. Aimee would kick Melanie to remind her to interpret, and they would both laugh.

The most memorable lesson of the year was called "Why Me?" The teacher, Darrin Palmer, had asked all the students to think of experiences where they asked themselves, "Why am I in this situation?" Before class, he had asked Aimee to share her story of deafness. Melanie was interpreting for Aimee that day.

Aimee stood up in front of about thirty students and told

her story: how the umbilical cord was wrapped around her neck when she was born, how her parents found out she was deaf when she was almost one, how not being able to hear had affected her life, how she hoped for the miracle of hearing at her baptism, how she waited after baptism to be able to hear, and how she felt peace after she realized that she could not hear. She realized that there was a reason that she was deaf, and that it was okay. She no longer questioned "why me?" about being deaf. Melanie struggled to interpret because she was overwhelmed by the story—even though she already knew it. The entire class was in tears. After the students left, Darrin Palmer, the teacher, approached Aimee in tears and said, "I didn't know your story. That's so awesome that you love who you are and you are grateful enough to overcome questioning 'why me?'" No one could forget the "Why Me?" lesson.

At Mountain View High School, one of Aimee's favorite teachers was Mr. Criman who coached football and track and taught English and theatre, including deaf theatre, which involved deaf students acting in plays like *Little Red Riding Hood* and *The Three Little Pigs*. In deaf theatre, the actors would sign an entire play, and oral interpreters would verbally explain and sign what the actors were saying for the audience. Expression and body language made the plays work, and Mr. Criman explained how Aimee was different from his other hearing and deaf students: "Aimee has a strong work ethic and is not easily distracted. She is gorgeous and skilled as an actress and is positive." Mr. Criman continued, "Somewhere along the line, Aimee decided that she was going to be successful at everything. I don't know when that happened. In any community, you have people who will use their problems as a crutch to not succeed, or rely on them to get gain. Whether it was conscious or not, Aimee knew that she had something to give. She always has had a strong affirmation that she is a child of God, and she transcends boundaries with her attitude."

After each performance, Mr. Criman would ask his students to provide oral critiquing, so they would know what they had done well and what to work on. Aimee's feedback was always very positive, but she would include constructive criticism—typically based on what the body language was saying. Deaf people are typically very expressive because they watch communication closely. Mr. Criman has said, "Aimee is a prodigy and could have gone professional [as a deaf actress] if she wanted to." Mr. Criman has worked with thousands of young people and claims that "successful students have grounded parents, or they have decided not to make the same mistakes their parents did. If you want to meet an amazing woman, meet Aimee's mom."

Aimee's father also played a role in Aimee's success. For example, in training for Junior Olympic Nationals in May 1999, Aimee was 16 years old. Nationals were held in Austin, Texas, which was hot and humid, and all the plants were green. Coaches from Division 1 universities throughout the U.S. came to nationals to recruit athletes. Cam took almost a week off of work to meet Patsy and Aimee in Austin. Aimee competed in all four events: vault, floor, bars, and beam. She stuck her routines, but earned her highest scores in floor and bars, where she medaled and earned a 36.65 overall, which placed her in 19th position all-around, out of about seventy girls at level 10. Aimee's success at level 10 launched her into training for Elite gymnastics. Aimee also had the opportunity to meet the head coach for UCLA, Valorie Kondos Field, who would become a key figure in Aimee's future.

One evening after eating at a restaurant, the family took a walk on the Congress Avenue Bridge, enjoying a beautiful sunset. Cam stopped on the bridge and signed, "I want to show you something. Just wait. Be patient." Cam looked around. At dusk, Mexican free-tailed bats started emerging from beneath the bridge, first a few hundred, and then thousands. Eventually, about 1.5 million bats blanketed the summer sky. These bats eat up to 20,000 pounds of insects, including agricultural pests, each night. Tourists line up on the bridge and gather in boats and in kayaks on the water to witness the largest urban bat colony in North America.

Cam took a minute to explain something to Aimee that she would never forget. Cam said, "You know, Aimee, bats are blind."

"Are they really blind?" Aimee said. "How do they get around?"

"They compensate for their blindness by developing other senses, like their hearing and smell." Cam said, "You are a little bit like those bats by being blind in one eye, and you have compensated for it by developing your other senses."

Although the notion that bats are blind is a myth, the lesson that Cam taught resonated with Aimee because it demonstrated his ongoing faith and support in her, and it showed how she has had to compensate for losses, find her own path, and compete on unequal ground.

Training at the elite level presented new challenges. Strength training focused on control and took about forty hours per week in the summer, and included climbing up a rope without using legs, pull-ups with legs in a horizontal position, and push-ups with legs in a vertical position above the body, tapping the head on the mat. One of the most challenging demands was holding a handstand for one minute with feet together. If the feet in the air separated or the hands on the mat moved—to restore balance—the sixty seconds started over.

Each morning started with a run. Once, as the athletes ran the bleachers, Aimee fell and hurt her knee, so she backed off, taking the last place in the line of girls—so as not to hold up anyone else. The team wove up and down the bleacher steps. Mary yelled, "Come on, Aimee. Don't come up with excuses." The morning sprinklers had doused part of the bleachers, making them slippery, and the bleachers were constructed of gray aluminum. With one eye, Aimee had no depth perception, so the steps lost their distinction in a sea of gray. Sprinting up and down these wet gray bleachers early in the morning with one eye was treacherous.

When the gauntlet of the bleachers ended, the team ran sprints on the field. Each time, Aimee came in first place. Speed was not an issue, and there were no excuses.

Eventually, Aimee tested to qualify for the Senior International Elite Competitions, the level required for Olympic athletes. In her first attempt in January 2000 at Olympus School of Gymnastics in Sandy, Utah, she passed compulsories with the support of her teammates. For example, on Aimee's floor routine, four team members would stand at the corners of the mat and give her nonverbal cues so she could keep time with her music. Despite passing compulsories, she failed to pass optionals at that time.

In April, for her second attempt, she flew to Rohnert Park outside of San Francisco with her coach Mary, her mother, and two teammates.

In the evening, Cam called for a family prayer—their routine when they were apart—and to share a scripture that he thought might help Aimee before her competition. Cam said the prayer while Patsy held the phone on her shoulder and signed the words to Aimee with both hands. Cam said he was sorry that he couldn't be there himself, and then he shared a favorite verse of scripture, which Patsy also signed: "And whoso receiveth you, there I will be also, for I will go before your face. I will be on your right hand and on your left, and my Spirit shall be in your hearts, and mine angels round about you, to bear you up." After the phone conversation, Aimee marked the verse in her own scriptures and reread it over and over. Aimee felt like everything would go well.

The next morning, Aimee started her testing. Each event went well, but her biggest challenge was the beam. The beam is made of wood, 16.4 feet long, 4.1 feet above the floor, and 4 inches wide. Female athletes execute runs, jumps, turns, and poses in routines that last about ninety seconds. A more difficult event could not be designed for someone who is deaf and blind in one eye because maintaining balance requires proper functioning of the inner ear and two eyes for depth perception. For a hearing person with clear vision to understand Aimee's challenge might involve spinning oneself dizzy, placing a patch over one eye, and doing tricks across an elevated path two inches narrower than the curb on the street.

During the competition, in the process of doing a switch side leap, Aimee's right foot started to slip off the beam. She felt herself tipping and thought: Oh no, I'm going off, face down. Then something happened. She felt two hands, one on the front of each shoulder, push her back up. Aimee remembered the promise—that angels on her right and left would bear her up. She felt a thrill throughout her body—and gratitude. She completed the routine without a hitch. At her dismount, with tearful eyes, she smiled at the judges.

Patsy missed the performance. She couldn't take the stress of watching. She couldn't breathe. As Aimee was about to begin, Patsy walked into a stall in the bathroom, closed the door, knelt down on the dirty floor, and prayed the whole time—that Aimee would be protected and do her best, and, if possible, achieve her dream. Less than two minutes into the prayer, Patsy heard a roaring cheer from the gym, and she tore out of the bathroom to join Aimee.

At the end of the competition, Mary, her coach, looked at all the judges' scores and told Aimee, "You passed." Aimee had reached the highest level in gymnastics: Senior International Elite, the level required to compete in the Olympics.

As Aimee, Patsy, and Mary ate salmon at Fisherman's Wharf after the event, Aimee exulted and thought about trying out for the Olympics. Mary said, "I have to be honest with you. You have not reached the Elite level yet. You passed compulsories in the winter and optionals in the spring, but they changed the requirement. You now have to pass both tests in the same season." Silence followed the bombshell. Aimee would have to retest for compulsories. After the day's success, the salmon lost its flavor.

The next compulsory test was held in Temecula in June. At that competition, Aimee performed well on all events again, but on the beam she fell, which she knew would be a .5 deduction. However, when that happened, she felt an impression: Do your best, and everything will be all right.

After the beam, Aimee waited for the judges to calculate the final scores. The judges gave them the news that Aimee did not qualify for the Elite level. Aimee was astonished. Wasn't her performance enough?

Moments later, the judges approached Mary to inform her that they made a calculation error on Aimee's scores. The correct score qualified Aimee to be a Senior International Elite gymnast. Mary and Aimee embraced each other. They could not have been happier.

More importantly, Aimee felt that God had helped her achieve her dreams, and her parents had paved the way.

Of the thousands of girls that Mary coached throughout her forty-nine-year coaching career, she noticed a unique quality that Aimee brought to her gym: she would never give up.

Aimee qualified to compete at the first of three events to qualify for the Olympic team, the U.S. Classic in Oklahoma, which involved about thirty-two girls, about fifteen of which would advance to Championships. About eleven of those athletes would advance to the Olympic trials, and finally seven would make the Olympic team.

Practices changed: they became like short meets in format, intensity, and pressure. Aimee was doing a double-and-a-half twist on the floor, and she suggested to Mary that she try a triple twist because she had plenty of power and it would earn bonus points. She had not done it much before, but she had done it on the tumble track, the ski floor, and into the pit. She felt like she could fly, and she was at the pinnacle of her career. Cam was in town for the weekend, and both he and Patsy watched Aimee practice from the parents' booth above. When they saw that Mary was approving the triple twist, Patsy stood and expressed her concern to Cam. They considered objecting because of the potential danger, but they kept their concern to themselves. After Aimee performed her roundoff and back handspring, she leapt high in the air for her triple twist, but she came up a little short—doing a 2 and ¾ twist—putting extra pressure on her legs. As she landed, she cried, dropped in agony to the mat, and her parents rushed down to her side. Aimee signed, "No. No. No." She saw her Olympic dream vanishing. She had dislocated her right knee—for a second time. The knee quickly turned red and swelled. Mary blamed herself for approving the triple twist. Aimee tried to console her by saying, "I asked you if I could do it. It was my fault," but Mary blamed herself. In the car on the way home, the Walkers cried.

Dr. Kimball found torn cartilage and, given the U.S. Classic coming up in a week, gave Aimee a cortisone shot to preserve her opportunity to compete. That evening, Grandpa Walker and Aimee's father gave her a blessing. In it, Grandpa Walker said, "You will be able to compete, and you will be an influence for good." Aimee had faith in her grandfather's blessing, but didn't know how it could happen.

After a week of light practices, prolonged icing, physical therapy, Advil, and fluid drained from her knee, Aimee, Patsy, and Mary flew to Tulsa, Oklahoma for the U.S. Classic. Aimee knew she had to compete in all four events to qualify for the Olympics, so she started to warm up on the floor, beam, and bars. The team doctor at the meet examined her knee, which was swollen and which sent excruciating pain throughout her body at each landing. He stopped her from competing. Aimee argued, "Please let me compete. I've been waiting for this moment for so many years. Please."

"No, that would not be a good idea," was the answer. "You may not compete."

"At least let me compete on the bars. Please. I'm begging you. I don't use my legs much for bars." The doctor considered the request but objected based on the dismount. Then, he thought more about it and said, "I'll clear you for the bars if you just do a fly-away layout for your dismount."

"But I want to do a double twist," replied Aimee.

"No, a fly-away layout only," said the doctor.

"Okay," said Aimee.

As soon as Aimee got the news that she was restricted to one event, she knew that she could not qualify for the 2000 Olympics in Sydney because to qualify for the Olympics, an athlete had to be an all-around contender, meaning competing in all four events. As the doctor taped, braced, and bandaged Aimee's knee for the bars, she reflected on her grandfather's blessing: she would compete and be an influence for good. How could she be an influence for good if she didn't make it to the Olympics?

At the competition, several prominent people took an interest in Aimee: Vanessa Atler, five-time senior national gymnastics champion; Bart Conner, 1984 Olympic gold medalist in gymnastics; Nadia Comaneci, 1976 gold medalist and first female to be awarded a perfect score of 10 in an Olympic gymnastics event; and Bela Karolyi, world renowned and controversial Olympic gymnastics coach. Bart explained to Aimee that the Fox Family Channel was making a documentary called "USA Gymnasts Go for the Gold" and asked if Aimee would participate. They interviewed Aimee, but Aimee thought nothing would come of it because she only competed in one event, didn't win, and didn't qualify for the Olympics. When the documentary came out, Aimee's story was woven throughout the two-hour special.

Aimee's journey had been a roller-coaster ride, but she drew comfort from how her grandfather's words were coming to pass: "You will be able to compete, and you will be an influence for good."

11 UCLA

In May 2002, as Aimee graduated from Mountain View High School, she reflected on two of her life goals: college and the Olympics. During her career, she had needed two knee surgeries, and they had made being an Olympic athlete very difficult. What to do next was the hardest decision of Aimee's life. By 2002, more than ten top universities had tried to recruit her. UCLA was ranked #1 in women's gymnastics, and they courted Aimee through football games, phone calls, dinners, and tours of the campus. They offered Aimee a full-ride scholarship. They also had five former Olympians on their team, and one of them was Jamie Dantzscher, with whom Aimee felt closest because they acted together in *Little Girls in Pretty Boxes* and trained together briefly at Charter Oak Gymnastics. Jamie also knew American Sign Language.

The head coach, Valorie Kondos Field, Miss Val to the gymnasts, explained that the entire team would learn sign language to make the environment work for Aimee. Valorie made it clear that UCLA wanted Aimee. Aimee fasted and prayed about what to do, and she decided to sign with UCLA, which meant putting her Olympic dream on the back burner and focusing on her college dream. After signing the NCAA papers to attend UCLA, Aimee felt calm—like she had done the right thing.

In 2000, Jamie Dantzscher had competed in Sydney, Australia, at the Olympics on the U.S. women's gymnastics team, and two experiences there jaded her. First, after the Romanians took the gold and the Russians took the silver, the Chinese edged out the U.S. team for the bronze. Ten years later, the International Federation of Gymnastics would strip the Chinese team of its bronze medal because one of its athletes had been too young (not turning 16 during the Olympic year), and the bronze would be given to the U.S. team. However, nothing in 2010 could erase the decade-long guilt Jamie felt for failing to medal, and she openly criticized Karolyi for how he handled the U.S. team. But there was an even more tragic event in Sydney for Jamie: a bus crashed into the taxi in which her father, John Dantzscher, and sister, Jennifer Dantzscher, were traveling. Jamie's father saw the bus coming, pushed Jamie's sister to the other side of the taxi, and covered her with his body, taking the brunt of the crash himself, nearly killing him through multiple injuries and leaving him disabled for life. Jennifer walked away with minor bruises. Jamie felt guilty about her gymnastics career bringing her family to Sydney where a bus destroyed her father's life.

During the time of the accident, Aimee was about to enter the 11th grade at Mountain View High School, and she and Patsy had kept in touch with Jamie and her mother, Joyce, through conversations and visits. The Walkers and the Dantzschers supported each other.

By the time Aimee entered UCLA as a freshman, Jamie was a senior, and she noticed what a bright light Aimee was on the gymnastics team, an inspiration to everyone, overcoming challenges and persevering, and gaining strength through her faith. Quite simply, Jamie said, "She has an inner peace. She gets life. Isn't that what we're all trying to do?"

Coach Valorie had been dancing professionally for The

Washington Ballet before UCLA hired her in 1982 to be a dance coach for the gymnastics team. She had no prior gymnastics experience. In 1990, UCLA gave her the head gymnastics coaching job because they saw tremendous leadership skills in her. She started her head coaching job by studying great coaches, and she approached her team with a coach's persona and tough clichés: "Go hard or go home" and "Winners make adjustments, and losers make excuses."

The entire time that she served as assistant coach, UCLA never finished lower than fourth place. However, in her first two years as head coach, gymnastics did so poorly that she realized she was in the wrong profession. On her way to see the athletic director to resign, she picked up Coach John Wooden's little blue book and read his definition of success: "Success is peace of mind that is the direct result of self-satisfaction in knowing you did your best to become the best that you are capable of becoming." She read it again and again. The word "you" stuck out to her: "Be the best that 'you' are capable of becoming." Don't try to be someone else. She realized that she was going about coaching in the wrong way. What did Valorie Kondos Field bring to the table as a coach? She took an inventory: she knew about discipline, sacrifice, preparation, perseverance, being a solo artist, and being a girl and feeling insecure between the ages of eighteen and twenty-two. She realized that she just needed to continue to do those things well and hire others to do the things she couldn't do well. She just needed to be herself.

One practical change that Valorie made was to drop her sarcasm. Once, her team sat her down and said, "We get it. You are trying to tick us off or embarrass us or hurt our feelings with sarcasm, but it's hard to deal with. We are tired from school, midterms, and practice, and the sarcasm just isn't funny." Valorie realized that she was coaching from her ego, which was not motivating them to improve. The sarcasm established dominance, but it did not establish trust and respect.

After Valorie started being authentic, she started enjoying her job. Then, her dynasty began. Her team won six national championships, and she was inducted into the UCLA Athletic Hall of Fame in 2010. Assistant Coach Milo said, "Val is the most insightful coach I have ever worked with."

When visitors enter Valorie's office, she asks them where they want to sit, the yellow loveseat sofa on the left or the black wooden chair on the right. Both belonged to the late Coach John Wooden—perhaps the greatest coach who ever lived—and his legacy lives on in her.

Each year, Valorie took her entire team to John's place to give them the opportunity to ask the legend some questions. When Aimee's team visited the Wooden home, she noticed that he lived in a small apartment condo. At least 100 awards and plaques were lined up on the floor leaning against the wall, running down the hall. In his spare bedroom, he had a hat from every professional baseball team that had sent him one—in four or five rows lined up neatly on the bed. In his bedroom, two hand-crafted cloth signs hung from the ceiling: one said, "John," and the other said, "Nell"—his wife, who died in 1985. The home was simple.

John, 94, sat in a chair at the end of his living room. There were only two couches, so most of the athletes sat on the floor. Aimee's father, Cam, sat next to John to interpret for Aimee. John began, "My favorite sport—other than basketball—is gymnastics. I like it so much because everything is on the line. Everything depends on you." He noted that it's an individual and a team sport. He explained that when he coached basketball, his work happened in practice. He presented the hardest conditions in practice, so when those situations came up in the games, his players had seen it a million times. When it came time to compete, it was up to the players to perform. His work was done. In fact, he explained that he had asked the athletic board at UCLA if he could sit in the stands during games—to sit with his wife—but the board denied his request.

He invited questions from the gymnastics team, and someone asked, "How does it feel to be the best and most famous coach in the world?"

John said, "I truly appreciate the accolades, but I don't believe I'm the best coach in the world. I think the best coach is in some little high school somewhere taking young boys and helping them to learn the fundamentals of basketball, to work hard, and to help them become better individuals. The best coaches change the lives of individuals in ways that have nothing to do with basketball."

Then John's phone rang. His answering machine went on. It was Bill Walton, one of his former players. John said, "He calls me every day. My relationships with my players are much deeper than basketball."

He explained that family was most important. He talked about his children and grandchildren. He talked about not fearing failure because failure provides the stepping-stones for success. He talked to the girls like they were his daughters.

John said, "I want to share a secret with you. I only carry two things in my wallet." He pulled out a picture of Nellie and him when they were dating in high school. They looked about fifteen.

Then he said, "When I was growing up, my favorite sport was baseball, and I wanted to become a professional baseball player." But his height was put to better use in basketball. He explained that a few years before, when he was in his 80s, he received a call from the Pittsburgh Pirates, asking him to come out to meet with them. He accepted the invitation, expecting to talk to and motivate the players. Instead, he sat in a room with the owner and managers. They asked him to be their team manager even though he had never played or coached baseball. John politely declined the offer but kept a very small newspaper clipping about it in his wallet.

At the end of the meeting, he said to Aimee, "You are one of my favorite athletes. I love watching you. Gymnastics is one of the hardest sports, and you are succeeding. It does my heart good." He came to almost every UCLA gymnastics meet.

Once an *LA Times* reporter was preparing an article about Coach John Wooden and why he liked gymnastics so much. He was interviewing both John Wooden and Valorie Kondos Field. Part of the article was about the success of UCLA gymnastics under the leadership of Valorie, and the reporter looked at her and said, "So you're becoming the next John Wooden?"

Before Valorie could respond, John said, "Why would she want to be another John Wooden when she can be such an amazing Valorie Kondos Field?"

In the fall of 2003, Aimee signed up for three classes at UCLA, which was a full-time load. All of her teachers during the first quarter allowed her to take oral tests in lieu of multiple-choice tests, and it's a common misconception that oral tests are easier than other tests. Oral tests for Aimee involved the teacher, Aimee, and an interpreter meeting, and the teacher asking a question, which the interpreter translated for Aimee. Aimee replied in American Sign Language, and the interpreter communicated in English what Aimee said. Aimee was not given multiple-choice answers; she had to generate the correct answer on her own. Although this method was harder for most, it worked better for Aimee because she was working in her native language, American Sign Language, not English. UCLA provided an interpreter for Aimee in all of her classes, and the first quarter went well.

During the second quarter, the most challenging class was anthropology. Aimee and her interpreter approached the professor, and Aimee explained that she was deaf and could not watch the interpreter and take notes at the same time. She asked, "Can I get a copy of the class notes or another student's notes?"

"No, you can't use another student's notes. You have to take them yourself," replied the professor.

Aimee explained again, "I'm deaf. I hear nothing. I can only use my eyes. I can't watch you and take notes. I'll miss what's going on. Hearing people can hear what is being said while they look down and take notes. I can't."

The teacher said, "No. I'm sorry. That wouldn't be fair to the other students."

"How can you not understand?" said Aimee.

"You're in college. You're a big girl. You need to do it yourself. The other kids are doing it," the professor responded.

Aimee didn't want to argue with the professor, so she signed, "Let's go," to the interpreter.

The interpreter said, "No. I'm going to stick up for you. I'm going to tell her the situation. Deaf culture is different than hearing. She needs to know that. I'm going to explain it to her," which she did, and the professor acquiesced and asked the class who would take notes for Aimee. One young woman volunteered, but it was still frustrating for Aimee because the notes did not match perfectly with what was being taught in the class.

Later, Aimee asked her anthropology professor if she could take the tests orally instead of in writing, and the professor said, "No."

Aimee explained that her other teachers during the first quarter allowed it.

"No. Period," was the answer.

Valorie and Aimee's academic counselor tried to intervene, but the professor would not allow accommodations. She was not swayed. She had tenure, so she had no fear of being fired.

A meeting ensued with everyone but the professor: Aimee, her parents, Valorie, the athletic counselor, and head of Students with Disabilities. Aimee's grades in her other classes were fine. The only question was anthropology. The group concluded that Aimee had to withdraw from the class to avoid a failing grade, which meant she would be a part-time student and ineligible for gymnastics. She had competed through the PAC-10 but would not be allowed to compete in everything leading up to nationals. Valorie and Aimee wept.

Later, the American Civil Liberties told the Walkers that they definitely had a case, but findings would not be announced until the following year. Nothing could be done to allow her to compete in 2004 postseason events.

Valorie said she would leave the scholarship open and available for Aimee for the following year.

Aimee withdrew from UCLA because she could not obtain the academic support that she needed, and in the 2003-2004 school year, UCLA had no deaf program. Not one American Sign Language (ASL) class had ever been offered at UCLA until 2012—eight years after Aimee's arrival—so they didn't have a program in place to support deaf students adequately. This was hard to believe given that ASL ranked 4th behind Spanish, German, and French as the most frequently studied language on U.S. college campuses, according to a *Daily Bruin* report by Asad Ramzanali. Further, Asad pointed out that in 2010, UCLA taught 50 languages—but not ASL—despite an 800 percent jump nationwide in enrollment in ASL courses since 1998.

At UCLA, Aimee competed on vault and bars, and she was the backup on the floor. Her favorite memory happened at the Pauley Pavilion in a meet against 4th-ranked University of Utah on January 5, 2004, prior to her withdrawal. One of Aimee's teammates got injured on the vault and couldn't do her floor routine. Valorie gave Aimee the look: It's your time. Get in there. Aimee had not even warmed up on the floor since she was a back-up and didn't expect to compete in that event, but she took off her warm-ups. Valorie said, "I can see in your eyes you are ready."

"I didn't even warm up. Do you think I'm ready?" said Aimee.

"Yep."

"I'm going to pay you back for this," Aimee said nervously.

"Calm down. Just have fun," said Valorie.

Aimee stretched out a little bit, stepped onto the mat, and saluted the judge. She knew the music started when Valorie gave her the cue to start. During the routine, Aimee felt amazing: warm, inspired, energetic, excited, and powerful. She stuck everything, and her knees didn't hurt. She jumped high, and her flips were beautiful. Her favorite part was the dancing between tricks because she could flirt with the crowd and involve them. She felt the love of the audience, and she danced with attitude, making a connection with them. After she finished her routine, she looked over at Valorie and gave her a little look of attitude. Valorie returned the look: I saw that. I know you've got it in you.

Not only did the UCLA fans cheer, but those wearing red, fans from Utah, stood up and cheered too. Many of them had heard about Aimee being deaf and blind in one eye, and coming back from injuries.

Aimee walked up to Valorie and said, "Thank you for giving me that opportunity, but please don't give it to me again without a warm-up!"

After the meet, the head coach for the University of Utah, Greg Marsden, was walking with Valorie through the tunnel as they left Pauley Pavilion. He had tried vigorously to recruit Aimee the year before and was a little bitter that she had chosen UCLA. He then heard that she was not doing so well due to her two knee surgeries. Greg said to Val, "I thought Aimee was struggling a little bit. What's up with that? She was amazing."

Aimee had always been a beautiful dancer. The first time that she competed on the floor in Pauley Pavilion, the place was packed, and Aimee brought the house to its feet. As a former ballet dancer, Valorie noticed Aimee's movement quality, which is usually inspired by music. Since Aimee can't hear the music, Valorie asked her what inspired her movement. Aimee said, "God."

Throughout her life, Aimee's faith has played a major role in her success. Valorie has noticed what sets Aimee apart from others: Aimee has made a choice to live a happy life, and she is not a victim. She is appreciative and joyful: God is good, and life is good. Aimee emanates light, which is infectious. Because she is not a victim, she is not self-absorbed. When someone on the team is frustrated or crying, Aimee is the first person to offer help. Because Aimee has overcome so many challenges, she has the tendency to pull people out of their self-pity. Valorie claims that Aimee has no disability: "Aimee's not deaf. She just can't hear. Why would she need two eyes, when she has one? She has no excuses."

Valorie's statement echoes words spoken to Aimee in a

patriarchal blessing seven years before she arrived at UCLA: "There are those who feel that you are handicapped, Aimee. This is not true: You are blessed with special talents and many will honor your name through the eternities because of the way you use these talents. . . . You will be a leaven among those with whom you associate."

During the national championships at Pauley Pavilion, Aimee was ineligible as a part-time student, so she had to sit in the stands with the spectators—even though her performances throughout the year had helped the team reach the national championships. Aimee tried not to cry in the stands. She felt alone. She had done her best, but she fell short in anthropology. She was on the outside now.

After the meet, she was allowed to come on the floor and join her teammates—the 2004 national champions. The team celebrated by crossing their arms and scratching their chests with their claws, the sign for bear or bruin—the UCLA mascot—a tradition that Valorie kept alive long after Aimee left.

12 Red Roses

Four years before Aimee's UCLA team won the national title, Aimee was a sophomore at Mountain View High School in Orem, Utah, where she had gone to train with Mary Wright. At that time, Derek Pond, who grew up in Provo, Utah, was serving in the California San Fernando Mission as an American Sign Language missionary, and the year was 2000. Derek Pond's name badge read "Elder Pond"—the title used by men serving full-time missions. Elder Pond and his companion, Elder Belshe, knocked on the door of the Walker home because they had been told that the Walkers had a deaf daughter and that the family knew American Sign Language. Because Aimee and Patsy were in Utah, Cam invited the missionaries to return for dinner on Thanksgiving when the family would be together in California.

On Thanksgiving, Aimee, who was seventeen and a half, couldn't help but notice how handsome both Elders were, but she focused on Elder Belshe because he was a deaf man and could sign so well. Elder Pond had been on his mission for a few months and was still acquiring signing skills. Elder Pond said, "My sister, Melissa, is a gymnast too," so they started talking about gymnastics. Before the missionaries left, Elder Pond opened up his napkin and said, "Will you sign this napkin? I want to send it to my sister." After Aimee signed Derek's napkin, she glanced up and noticed Elder Pond's dimples and smile.

Elder Pond and Aimee exchanged two brief, platonic letters in the following months.

On March 10, 2002, Aimee's 19th birthday, she was finishing her senior year at Mountain View High School in Orem and had flown to California with her mom for the weekend to accept a speaking invitation in Santa Clarita. As Aimee sat on the stand waiting to speak, she noticed Elder Pond, who was serving as a zone leader, a missionary leadership position, assigned to work in the Solemint Ward, a congregation on the east side of Santa Clarita. He walked in late with a young man he was teaching. Elder Pond looked at Aimee and signed, "Sorry, we're late. Do you remember me?" Of course, Aimee did, and she felt a little embarrassed. After Aimee told her story through her mother as interpreter, Elder Pond approached Aimee. They chatted for a few minutes. Elder Pond explained that he was finishing his mission in two weeks, and he signed, "Would you like to attend my homecoming in Provo?"

"Yes," replied Aimee, excited about the invitation. Then, all those around Aimee sang "Happy Birthday" to her, and Elder Pond signed the song as he sang it.

Elder Pond had still not focused on Aimee romantically. When Elder Pond had left on his mission, he had a girlfriend, and he wrote her faithfully during the first year of his mission until he received a package from her. In it, he found all the letters that he had written to her, and each one was unopened. She included a "Dear John" letter that explained, "I'm now married and pregnant." Although this type of news would have been devastating to most missionaries, Elder Pond took it in stride and completely refocused on his mission.

Back in Utah a few weeks later, Patsy and Aimee attended Elder Derek Pond's homecoming, after which they went to the Pond home to eat and celebrate Derek's successful mission and safe return home. Derek's mother, Judy, put her arm around Aimee and took her around to meet all the relatives, one by one. Before the event ended, Derek secured Aimee's email address. As Patsy and Aimee left the Pond home, Derek signed, "I love you."

Aimee didn't know what to think because—although it's common in Deaf culture to sign "I Love You"—she usually reserved that sign for her family, but she waved, "I love you too."

In the car, Aimee said, "Did you see that he signed 'I love you' to me?"

"Oh, no, no, no, just friends, trust me," replied Patsy, thinking, Calm down!

Three days later, Derek asked Aimee on a date—bowling on the BYU campus. Aimee had been on dates before, but it was wonderful to be on a date with someone who signed so well, and his signing had improved tremendously since they first met at Thanksgiving dinner in California. After bowling three strikes in a row, Derek celebrated by doing the James Brown splits to reveal how flexible he was, and then Aimee did the splits. They hit it off, laughing and talking throughout the evening. That date was Aimee's favorite date of her life because Derek spoke her language, and he was so respectful and polite. He was very patient, and he spent a lot of time listening to Aimee.

Derek and Aimee dated each other exclusively for almost two years, and in that period they spent time in both Utah and California. On February 14, 2004, Derek took Aimee on a date to an Italian restaurant in Santa Monica, California. After dinner, they took a walk on the beach near the pier. Aimee was cold, so Derek put his jacket around her. As they walked, Aimee, noticing some lights in the sand in the distance, said, "What's that?"

"I don't know. Let's go see," said Derek.

They came upon a set of about a dozen short candles—each recessed several inches in the sand—together forming a circle with flames flickering in the evening breeze. In the middle of the circle lay two-dozen long-stem red roses tied together with a red ribbon, resting on a red and white blanket.

"Wow. Did someone just leave this? It's amazing that it hasn't been destroyed," said Aimee.

"It's for you," said Derek. "Happy Valentine's Day." Derek's mom, brother, and sister had set it up as Derek and Aimee ate dinner earlier that evening.

Derek and Aimee both stepped over the candles, sat on the blanket, and talked about their relationship and their goals. After a while, Derek asked Aimee to stand up. As Aimee stood in the circle of candles looking at the roses, the moonlight glistened on the shoulders of the waves. Derek knelt on one knee, unveiled a black box from his pocket, and signed, "Will you marry me?"

Aimee's eyes shifted from Derek's dimples to the smooth solitaire diamond ring set in white gold and back to Derek. "Yes," Aimee signed, beaming. Derek placed the ring on Aimee's finger.

They kissed!

They had discussed marriage many times, and they were excited about the prospect of starting their own family. They felt that they could accomplish anything together. They hugged, and kissed some more.

Without Aimee knowing it, Derek had spoken to Aimee's parents five months prior to ask for their blessing on their marriage, and both Cam and Patsy approved of the marriage but asked Derek to wait until after the spring semester so as not to jeopardize Aimee's UCLA scholarship.

Their only concern was how Aimee's parents would take the news. Aimee was supposed to be home by midnight each Saturday, and Derek and Aimee arrived at 12:30 a.m. with butterflies about sharing their new plans. Derek suggested that he wait in the living room while Aimee approached her parents, who would probably be asleep in their bed. Aimee walked into her parents' bedroom in the dark and tapped her mother on the shoulder. Cam quickly ripped the quilt back and grabbed Aimee's left hand. As soon as he felt the rock, he yelled a question in crescendo: "Where is Derek? Where is Derek?

Where is Derek?"

Cam's face was red.

In the conversation that followed, Cam made it clear that he supported the wedding, but his request for them to wait until the semester ended had not been honored. Aimee's grades had already started dropping in anthropology because the professor would make no accommodations for Aimee, and the gymnastics team was close to securing a national title. The Walkers felt that any distraction could cost her the UCLA scholarship.

Derek, who had been home from his mission and dating Aimee for almost two years, wanted to marry her. During the next few hours, Cam grilled Derek with questions peppered by lectures, and Patsy had to remind them several times to continue signing to allow Aimee to follow the conversation. Aimee had never seen her father behave this way before, and the conversation lasted until 4:45 a.m.

After a short night, the Walkers woke up and went to church with Derek and his family who were in town visiting. While socializing at church, Derek's mother, Judy, stood up and announced that her son, Derek Pond, was now engaged to Aimee Walker—with a proud smile on her face. Patsy cried. She shrank in her chair, said nothing, and tried to hide the eruption inside of her. The women gathered around Judy to share in the joyous details of the engagement, and one of them said, "Forget the scholarship. Marriage is much better," which drove a stake into Patsy's heart because she had sacrificed everything for Aimee's gymnastics career. After church, Patsy invited Judy and her family over for dinner. Patsy made a point of not making one negative comment, and she felt confident that she would never allow anyone to understand the pain associated with this untimely engagement.

Since high school, Aimee and her best friend Melanie had dreamed of a double wedding when they turned twenty-five, but Aimee's boyfriend proposed when she was twenty-one, and Melanie's boyfriend proposed nine years later. Aimee and Melanie spent the evening before her wedding talking. Melanie questioned Aimee: Are you sure Derek is the right person for you? Will he be able to take care of you financially? And on and on. They talked until about 3:00 a.m.

Grandma Clinger insisted on paying for Aimee's wedding dress, which looked traditional and elegant. It had a square neckline, tapered waist, a single row of buttons down the back, sheer sleeves, and a floor-length skirt with a flowing train. Crystal sequins sparkled along the neckline and shoulders. Aimee's hair was pulled up, and her curls bounced as she moved—more like a goddess than a mortal.

On Saturday, August 14, 2004, Grandpa Walker married Derek and Aimee, sealing them together as a couple forever in the Los Angeles Temple where Aimee's parents were married, where Derek's parents were married, and where Grandpa Walker had served as Temple President. After Derek and Aimee kissed, Aimee reflected on what it might mean to be married forever. She had attended wedding ceremonies of friends where the minister had ended the ceremony with " . . . until death do you part." Aimee felt comfort in knowing that she was married ". . . for time and for all eternity." She felt love and a new sense of responsibility.

After the hard work leading up to the marriage day, Patsy felt a change of heart and peaceful in the temple, and she thought, This must be what heaven is like.

At the reception, Derek danced with Aimee while a live band performed "When You Say Nothing at All," which held a special meaning for Aimee because it was the first song to which they danced when Derek and Aimee attended the MORP dance (prom spelled in reverse) her senior year in high school. As they danced, Derek held Aimee with one hand and, in tears, signed the lyrics with the other:

It's amazing how you can speak right to my heart
Without saying a word you can light up the dark
Try as I may I can never explain
What I hear when you don't say a thing

The smile on your face let's me know that you need me
There's a truth in your eyes saying you'll never leave me
The touch of your hand says you'll catch me wherever I fall
You say it best, when you say nothing at all . . .

Then came the opportunity for Aimee's dance with her father. The way that Cam and Aimee moved to "Butterfly Kisses" in the father-daughter dance reflected their life-long relationship. Cam had a sense of humor, and he knew how to dance: spinning, twisting, and dipping—joyful all the while. Cam had always drawn Aimee's attention away from the challenges of life and toward the fun and positive side of things—which any woman lucky enough to dance with him could experience in his arms. Now, it was Aimee's turn, and the image of that brief dance with her father on her wedding night would glow in her memory long after the dance ended.

After Derek and Aimee cut the wedding cake, Derek gingerly placed a piece of cake in Aimee's mouth. In turn, Aimee took a piece of wedding cake and quickly pressed it into each cheek and on to his nose for good measure—as if she couldn't find his mouth. Aimee always knew what to do in the spotlight, and she entertained everyone—again. After she saw what she had done to Derek's face, she backed up, placing her hand over her mouth to conceal her delight. She had been trained to push the limits, and Derek now looked like he came straight from the circus.

As Derek and Aimee began their married life together, they agreed that they would not have children for three years because a pregnancy would terminate her scholarship.

In Provo, Utah, Coach Brad Cattermole and Assistant Coach Dawn Cattermole, women's gymnastics coaches at BYU, heard from Valorie Kondos Field that Aimee was not competing, that UCLA had no American Sign Language program, and that UCLA couldn't provide the academic support that Aimee needed. Brad assured Aimee that BYU offered the support that UCLA could not provide, and he offered her a BYU scholarship. The decision for Aimee was difficult because UCLA was ranked #1 while BYU was not even in the top ten, but it had the support she needed to enjoy success: a strong American Sign Language program, excellent interpreters, and all the needed accommodations. She would have to red-shirt (withdraw from competition) for one year, but she signed with BYU.

At BYU, Aimee had several significant experiences. After winning 1st place on bars for BYU against Utah State during her first year of eligibility in 2006, the season was off to a great start. Then, on February 10, 2006, in heavy snow, the gymnastics team, including coaches and trainers, took the bus to Cedar City to compete at Southern Utah University (SUU). Derek could not attend because he had two full-time jobs and was also a student at Utah Valley University. As the meet started, Aimee could see members of her family watching from the stands. She warmed up on the bars and vault. On the vault, she did a Yurchenko full, but when she landed, her ankle popped. She tried to get up, but couldn't. Brad ran over and picked her up. She was crying and thinking, I can't believe another injury. I can't go through this. Why did this have to happen? I just barely came back, got my eligibility, and worked through a whole year of red-shirting, watching everybody else compete and have such a fun time. What the heck? How did this happen?

Gaye, her trainer, taped and iced her ankle and elevated her leg. No one else on the team came to her. They were all getting ready to compete. She felt alone. Gaye said, "Can you move your ankle?"

"No," signed Aimee.

After the meet, Aimee stayed behind because she was crying and didn't want to bring down her teammates. She struggled on crutches to make her way up through the stadium, so her brother, Danny, carried her. He said, "Remember your favorite saying: 'Never, Never, Never give up.' You'll come back with more power." Danny dropped her off at the front of the bus, but the only seats left were at the back of the bus. No one moved. No one said anything. She worked her way to the back of the bus on one leg. The rest of the team was consoling Kendra, who had injured her knee at the meet. Aimee sat alone, and no one came to console her on the bus. She tried to talk to her teammates a little, but nothing came of it. She felt isolated. She tried to do some homework, but she felt too depressed to study. She texted her mom back and forth during the long 4-hour drive back to Provo.

Aimee also texted her husband, Derek, to tell him about the injury and see if he could pick her up. He said that he would, but he was half asleep when he sent the text. Derek then asked his mother, Judy, if she could pick up Aimee because she was already going to pick up Melissa, her daughter who was able to exhibition at the meet, and Derek needed to be at work in the morning.

When the bus arrived, Judy was there to pick up Aimee and Melissa. Judy was excited about Melissa's opportunity to be involved in the exhibition, but she never consoled Aimee about her ankle injury. Aimee sat in the front seat and cried on the way. She texted Derek to see if he was awake, and he had been sleeping. Aimee asked if he could come to the car to get her bag and carry her in because of her injury. He said, "My mom can help you." Aimee thought, Wow. This is so strange.

Judy carried Aimee's bag to the door and came back to help her walk to her apartment, which involved descending five stairs slowly. She left her bag outside the front door and crawled on her hands and knees to her bed.

She said, "Derek, please help me." Derek, who had been working as a unit assistant in an operating room and as an American Sign Language interpreter at a university and attending college, finally woke up. He propped up a pillow beneath her leg and went back to sleep. In the middle of the night, Aimee woke up in pain. "Can you get me some Advil and water?" she said to Derek.

"No, you go. You go," replied Derek, who was half asleep. He had to work at 6:30 a.m.

Aimee thought, Oh, my gosh! She decided not to wake him up again.

She crawled across the floor, got a chair because she was too short to reach the medication, climbed up on the chair with one leg, grabbed the painkillers, filled a cup with water, and took the medicine. Then she filled the cup with water again, put a lid on it, and crawled back to bed with the cup and medicine so she could take another dose later in the night without having to crawl back to the kitchen.

That night, she didn't know what Dr. Kimball would tell her following the x-rays: "It looks like someone took a sledge hammer to your ankle: it's broken into many pieces." During surgery, Dr. Kimball placed two permanent screws in her ankle and grafted in bone from a cadaver.

The first day Aimee returned to the gym after surgery, she rolled in with her right knee on a scooter. Assistant Coach Dawn told the whole team that she was sorry that Aimee's gymnastics career was over. She was finished. She would still be part of the team as assistant trainer and coach and help out.

Aimee could not believe what she was saying. Aimee thought, Who gave her permission to say that to the team? I haven't even discussed my future with her or Brad. It broke Aimee's heart.

After the girls started to practice, Aimee confronted Dawn and said, "Why, why would you say that? What were you thinking? Why do you think that gymnastics is over for me?"

"Well, I heard from Dr. Kimball that your injury was so bad that you will walk with a limp. He is not expecting a full recovery," she said.

"No," Aimee replied. "Look at my knees. Two knee surgeries. People thought I would never recover from that. You don't know. I came back. Didn't I do it? Through great physical therapy and rehab. You tell them, 'Aimee won't come back.' No way. You don't know me very well. I'm not finished with my gymnastics career." Brad smiled.

"Please, please talk with me first. That made me feel terrible," said Aimee.

"You're right," said Dawn. "I should have talked with you

first. Gaye had just told us how damaged your ankle was and how challenging it was for Dr. Kimball to fix it, but you're right."

"I'm going to take some time off and see my physical therapist," Aimee said.

Brad smiled again and said, "I know who you are. You're Aimee Walker. I know you're going to come back."

In California between semesters, Jeff Beckondam, Aimee's physical therapist, worked her behind off. Aimee would lie on her stomach on a bench with her knee bent and ankle in the air while Jeff rotated and stretched it. He said, "Are you ready for pain? I think you can take it. You might want to bite on this towel." As Jeff rotated the ankle, broke up scar tissue, and rubbed around the screws, Aimee bit into the towel and cried. Aimee also strengthened her ankle by balancing on a gel ball.

Physical therapists view athletes at a unique time—when injuries threaten their careers—and Jeff noticed what set Aimee apart from his other athletes: "Most high-level injured athletes operate from fear: Will I come back? Aimee operates from self-confidence: When I come back. . . ." In a twenty-eight-year career, working with athletes of all levels, Jeff explained, "Aimee is in the top five athletes I have rehabbed in terms of commitment and work ethic, not to mention her delightful personality."

Back in Utah after eight months, Aimee returned to Dr. Kimball for a check-up. He examined her walking, jumping, and squatting, using a variety of assessments. He said, "I see no difference in your ankles. Wow, Aimee, you are very, very lucky. This is very rare—to come back from this type of injury." He started telling his colleagues about it. The recovery appeared to be 100%.

Aimee started training with the team and from then on focused on bars. Her ankle was taped and braced, but landings still hurt.

One week after her injury at SUU, Aimee asked Derek why he wasn't more helpful the night she came home with a broken ankle. Derek explained that he wanted her to become more independent. Three weeks after the injury, Derek apologized.

During the beginning of her senior year, Aimee sustained a shoulder injury. Dr. Kimball told her, "This injury will probably require a surgery. You are in your senior year, and you have given it your all. You have fought through injuries that would stop anyone, but there is no way that you could have a surgery and come back in that short amount of time. No way." Aimee objected to being told she couldn't compete—as she had done in the past—but the weight of her limp body as she hung on the bars, without doing anything, sent excruciating pain through her frame. She had taken a punishment during her gymnastics career, and the injuries had added up: sprained toes, broken toes, dislocated fingers, ripped hands, sprained wrist, broken fingers, broken foot, sprained ankle, fractured ankle with major surgery (2 screws in ankle), pulled hamstring, sprained neck, bruised eye, bruised sternum, split chin, broken tailbone, shin splints, pulled knee tendon, pulled Achilles tendon, dislocated elbow, subluxation on shoulder, dislocated knees, two major knee surgeries (2 screws in each knee), strained lower back, and subluxation of rib.

Aimee felt sad that her gymnastics career ended like this. She had invested all of her talent and effort into the sport, and her parents had sacrificed their time, energy, and money to help Aimee become an elite gymnast. Retirement was painful.

The silver lining in Aimee's career-ending injury came as she focused more on school. Although she still attended the full practices as an assistant coach and trainer, she had more free time for homework, and she worked harder than ever in her classes. Her overall GPA through her junior year was 3.46, but her senior-year GPA rose to 3.78.

Her major was Recreation Management and Youth Leadership, and she was also doing a coaching internship for All-American Gymnastics club. This experience gave her the first opportunity to coach young athletes, and she learned how frustrating being a coach is. She had never thought about that. She would say to her young athletes, "No, that's not right. Go back. Try it again." Some of them wouldn't listen. Aimee thought, Is this how it's going to be with my own children? The internship helped Aimee to understand the importance of patience and relationship building. Aimee learned to help the young athletes overcome their fears of trying harder tricks through the trust that she established with them. She also learned that each young athlete was unique and had to be approached differently. Aimee was able to communicate without an interpreter most of the time during her internship because many of the young girls had taken American Sign Language classes, which were popular in local schools, and Aimee was able to demonstrate how to perform skills visually.

At one BYU practice in the spring of Aimee's senior year, Brad told Aimee that she needed to attend the basketball game that night. In fact, the entire women's gymnastics team would be there. Brad told Aimee that she was getting an award, but she didn't understand what award. Aimee went alone—without her husband, without her parents, and without an interpreter—just with her team. She tried to text her family, but the battery on her phone had died. She had no other way of contacting them at the time.

Lena, an assistant coach, drove Aimee to the Marriott Center, and Aimee was wearing her gymnastics warm-up sweats. The National Association of Collegiate Gymnastics Coaches for Women granted Aimee and several other athletes the All-American Scholar Athlete award, a beautiful transparent trophy with "BYU All-American 2007" etched above the image of a cougar. Aimee reflected on the award: Who would have thought this would happen to me? After all the academic problems at UCLA and having to leave that university for academic reasons, after all the injuries in the gym and challenges in the classroom, who would have thought this would happen to me? The All-American Scholar Athlete award. She valued it like an Olympic gold medal. She considered her career ending this way to be a blessing.

She wished her family could enjoy this academic award with her—and join her in a picture.

On Aimee's graduation day from college in April 2008, the extended family went out to eat. Aimee ordered a mango chicken salad, her favorite, but she couldn't eat a bite. She felt sick. Her brother, Jamie, asked, "Are you pregnant?"

"No, no, I just don't feel well."

The next day, Aimee took a pregnancy test. It was positive. She didn't believe it, so she took another test. It was positive too. At first, Aimee told only three people: Derek, her mother, and Grandpa Walker because he was dying. When she shared the news with Grandpa Walker, he just smiled because he could no longer speak. Aimee said, "If we have a boy, we are going to name him after you." Grandpa smiled again. He had performed the marriage ceremony for Derek and Aimee four years earlier. Two months after hearing of Aimee's pregnancy, he died.

Aimee's pregnancy provided her an opportunity to reflect on the gift of life. Twenty-five years earlier in a hospital in Tarzana, Dr. Barlow had examined and tested Aimee when she was a newborn. He had declared, "She probably won't be a ballerina. She probably won't be a rocket scientist either." He was right. Instead, she had become a gymnast, and—despite being born deaf and blind in her right eye—she had overcome challenge after challenge, setback after setback to rise to become an International Elite gymnast—a feat no other athlete with comparable disabilities had accomplished in the history of the sport. She was also the first person in her family to graduate from college, and Aimee's family and community had supported her in her goals.

When Aimee's father, Cam, blessed Aimee as a baby, he said, "You will be a light to the world" and will have "a special compassion that will draw others to you and allow you to touch others." Soon, Aimee's husband would bless their first child. What challenges might their baby face? What talents might their baby have? What role would Aimee play in helping their child to blossom? Aimee would continue to face new challenges with the same qualities she always had: determination, faith, and optimism.

Epilogue

Aimee is currently a certified USA gymnastics instructor. She is also in the process of qualifying to judge gymnastics at the Senior International Elite level—the level at which she competed and the level required to serve as judge at the Olympics.

Derek and Aimee have also opened Champion Sports Center in Saratoga Springs, Utah, which serves more than 80 athletes between the ages of 15 months and 18 years. They are developing it into a world-class center for gymnastics and physical therapy.

Aimee continues to inspire others through motivational talks to groups of all types.

On January 23, 2009, Callie Noel Pond was born, followed by Kaiden Jensen Pond on August 31, 2010; Brian Russell Pond, on June 24, 2012; and Justin Aaron Pond on March 5, 2014. All four children learned to sign before they learned to speak.

Motherhood required an adjustment for Aimee. As the youngest in her family, she had never babysat siblings. As an Olympic hopeful during her teenage years, she never had time for babysitting. She quickly learned how to change diapers with her first child.

Aimee always wondered if her children would be deaf or hearing, but all of them hear well. Raising children as a deaf mother requires having special monitors. When one of her babies cries in another room at night, a monitor picks up the sound and sets off a light. At nighttime, the monitor will activate a vibration pad on Aimee's pillow that wakes her up so she can attend to her child.

Aimee feels that being a Mom is even better than being a gymnast because she and her children learn from each other. Aimee now appreciates her own mother much more than she used to. Aimee's husband and her own children are the most important things in the world to her.

Kaiden, her second child, was born in just two hours of labor with subglottic stenosis—narrowed breathing passage—acid reflux, and low muscle tone. In addition, his head had an indentation, and it was always turned to the side—with his left ear firmly leaning on his left shoulder. Derek noticed that Kaiden breathed uneasily, so the doctor kept him in the hospital for several days after his birth for observation and tests.

After Kaiden went home, his breathing problems increased over the next two years—with many visits to various doctors for steroid inhalers, asthma treatments, check-ups, and tests. The low point came just before Kaiden's second birthday. Aimee was still recovering from the birth of Brian, their third child, three weeks prior. Derek and Aimee had just moved to California two weeks earlier for Derek to attend Western University of Health Science, and Derek was recovering from an appendectomy the preceding week. Suddenly, Kaiden couldn't breathe and turned blue. Derek and Aimee rushed him to the hospital in Chino Hills, and from there an ambulance rushed Aimee and Kaiden to Loma Linda University Children's Hospital. The staff required that Aimee sit in the front seat of the ambulance, and they would not allow her to look back at Kaiden.

At the hospital, the doctor and several nurses ran a battery of tests on Kaiden and bombarded Aimee with a set of questions about Kaiden's condition and history. The hospital had no interpreter, Derek was outside in the van with the baby and Callie, and Aimee's parents had not yet arrived. Aimee tried to write answers to the doctor's questions on a piece of paper and make simple signs with her hands and hold Kaiden, who couldn't breathe and wouldn't be comforted from all the unsuccessful attempts by nurses to start an IV. Aimee broke down in tears.

After Derek joined Aimee, the doctor made it clear that Kaiden needed a tracheotomy and would not be able to speak. Although Kaiden knew American Sign Language well, the news devastated Derek and Aimee. After the doctor performed the surgery, Aimee had to learn how to suction the tracheostomy tube multiple times both day and night and change it on a weekly basis—all in a perfectly sterile environment to avoid lung infection.

Once, a playmate ripped Kaiden's tracheostomy tube out of his throat, so Aimee has had to monitor Kaiden and curious children around him carefully.

After two years of progress with Kaiden's breathing through his tracheostomy tube, he was finally able to blow out a candle at Callie's 6th birthday party. The family went crazy with delight. After two and a half years with a tracheotomy and after 5 surgeries, Kaiden is now tracheotomy free, breathing normally, and able to speak.

Aimee prayed fervently for two things in her life: for the ability for her to hear and for the ability for Kaiden to breathe normally. God answered both prayers. The first answer was no: her hearing would not be restored in this life, and that answer came with a feeling of peace—peace that all would be okay. The second answer was yes: Kaiden recovered completely.

After Kaiden's recovery, Aimee knelt down privately. Tears streamed down her cheeks, and she paused to find the right words. Then, she expressed gratitude to God eloquently in her own language.

Acknowledgements

I'm very grateful to so many who have made all the difference in my life: My wonderful Grandpa and Grandma Walker for driving me to class when I had a broken ankle. Without their help, I could not have graduated from BYU. Thank you to all of the Walker Family. Thank you to my dear Granddad and Grandma Clinger. I miss you and love you. Thank you to all the Clinger Family. A special thanks to my sweet cousin, Heather Pack Thompson, who interpreted for me so many times. Thanks to my Uncle Aaron Clinger for making donations to help pay for my gymnastics. For my Aunt Debra Clinger Jensen— through her creative suggestion, I got my start in gymnastics when my cousin Rahny hurt her ankle and couldn't continue on with the pre-paid class. I'm so grateful to my mother-in-law and father-in-law, Judy and Martin Pond, who are always there for me, and the entire Pond family, especially my sister-in-law, Kristin. To my brothers, Danny and Jamie, for all of their love, support, and sacrifice throughout the years. To my Mother and Father, for being there for all of the joys and sorrows every second of every day, and a special thanks to my Mom Patsy, who has been my ears and my voice since the beginning.

Thank you to all my teammates through the years on all my teams: Valley College, Santa Monica Gymnastics Center, Gymnastics Olympica, Charter Oaks Gymnastics, Golden State Gymnastics, Olympus School of Gymnastics, Scats Gymnastics, UCLA, and BYU.

Thank you to all my phenomenal coaches who believed in me, taught me, and encouraged me towards success: Dawn Salizar, Al and Linda Luber (Santa Monica Gymnastic Center), Erik Betts, Rafael Beer (photographer), Jennifer Mickschl Jordan, Fritz Reiter (Gymnastics Olympica), Hal Halverson (Golden State Gymnastics), Mary Wright (Olympus School of Gymnastics), Ron Howard, Chris Caso, Valerie Kondos Field (UCLA), and Brad and Dawn Cattermole (BYU).

Thank you to all of my teachers, interpreters, and tutors along the way. Special thanks to Carl and Suzie Kirchner, Nancy Fink, Jacqueline Barr, Steve Silverman, Nancy Kelly, Raquel Barr, Bekah Beachley, and Jodi Young Philip.

Thank you to all of my wonderful friends who gave me extra support and strength: Melanie Gurney Sell, Karen Freeman, Krystle Wong, Lena Johnson Starr, Jamie Dantzscher, Joyce Dantzscher, Elena Lozano Futter, Ann Stires, Harry Caratti and the Grandsons of Italy in America, Ray from Hawaii, Catherine Bartl Thomas, Jaune Osborne Curtis, Bishop James and Nori Johnson, Loni Levitt, Lucky Jeans, Sallie Weaver (GK Elite), David Hasselhoff, Nellie Kim, Kathy Johnson, Jeffrey T. Bekendam, John Wooden, all of my wonderful friends and family at church and school, especially all of those who learned sign language so they could communicate with me, and to Adam Kempler for his continued interest in my story. And to my fabulous husband, Derek, whom I love so much, and who has been by my side for these many years, and for our four beautiful children: Callie, Kaiden, Brian and Justin. They are the love of my life and bring me all the joy and happiness in the world.

— Aimee Walker-Pond

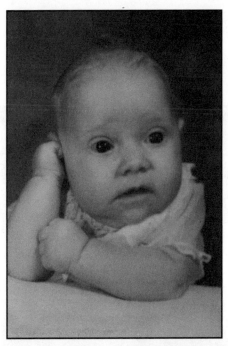

Aimee at 1 week old

Aimee and Cam

Jamie, Danny, and Aimee

The Walkers: Danny, Cam, Aimee, Patsy, and Jamie

David Hasselhoff and Aimee

Coach Hal Halverson and Aimee going surfing in Hawaii

Photo by Rafael Beer ©

Photo by Rafael Beer ©

Patsy kissing Aimee

Aimee modeling for GK Elite Sportswear

Aimee's high school graduation photo

Aimee competing for UCLA

Aimee competing for UCLA

UCLA wins 2004 national championship

Aimee competing for BYU

Aimee while at BYU

Derek and Aimee's engagement photo

Aimee opening lingerie at her wedding shower

Aimee on her wedding day

Derek and Aimee
To view more photos and video, visit www.impact-publishing.com